Letts
gets you through

MATHS
QUICK PRACTICE TESTS

Ages 10–11

11+ MATHS

FOR CEM

QUICK PRACTICE TESTS

FAISAL NASIM

Contents

ACKNOWLEDGEMENTS

The author and publisher are grateful to the copyright holders for permission to use quoted materials and images.

All images are © HarperCollins*Publishers*

Every effort has been made to trace copyright holders and obtain their permission for the use of copyright material. The author and publisher will gladly receive information enabling them to rectify any error or omission in subsequent editions. All facts are correct at time of going to press.

Published by Letts Educational

An imprint of HarperCollins*Publishers* Limited

1 London Bridge Street

London SE1 9GF

ISBN: 9781844198931

First published 2017

10 9 8 7 6 5 4 3 2 1

© HarperCollins*Publishers* Limited

All rights reserved. No part of this publication may be reproduced, stored in a retrieval system, or transmitted, in any form or by any means, electronic, mechanical, photocopying, recording or otherwise, without the prior permission of Letts Educational.

British Library Cataloguing in Publication Data.

A CIP record of this book is available from the British Library.

Author: Faisal Nasim

Commissioning Editor: Michelle I'Anson

Editor and Project Manager: Sonia Dawkins

Cover Design: Paul Oates

Text Design, Layout and Artwork: Q2A Media

Production: Paul Harding

Printed by Martins the Printers

Please note that Letts is not associated with CEM or The University of Durham in any way. This book does not contain any official questions and it is not endorsed by CEM or The University of Durham.

Our question types are based on those set by CEM, but we cannot guarantee that your child's actual 11+ exam will contain the same question types or format as this book.

CEM, Centre for Evaluation and Monitoring and *The University of Durham* are all trademarks of The University of Durham.

About this book

Familiarisation with 11+ test-style questions is a critical step in preparing your child for the 11+ selection tests. This book gives children lots of opportunities to test themselves in short, manageable bursts, helping to build confidence and improve the chance of test success.

It contains 45 tests designed to build key numeracy skills.

- Each test is designed to be completed within a short amount of time. Frequent, short bursts of revision are found to be more productive than lengthier sessions.

- CEM tests often consist of a series of shorter, time-pressured sections so these practice tests will help your child become accustomed to this style of questioning.

- If your child does not complete any of the tests in the allocated time, they may need further practice in that area.

- We recommend your child uses a pencil to complete the tests, so that they can rub out the answers and try again at a later date if necessary.

- Children will need a pencil and a rubber to complete the tests and some spare paper for rough working. They will also need to be able to see a clock/watch and should have a quiet place in which to do the tests.

- Your child should **not** use a calculator for any of these tests.

- Answers to every question are provided at the back of the book, with explanations given where appropriate.

- After completing the tests, children should revisit their weaker areas and attempt to improve their scores and timings for those tests.

Download a free progress chart, maths glossary and topic checklist from our website

letts-revision.co.uk/11+

Test 1

You have **5 minutes** to complete this test.

You have **10 questions** to complete within the given time.

Draw a line in the box below the correct answer.

EXAMPLE

Round 32,134 to the nearest 100.

32,100	32,000	31,000	32,500

---

(1) $743 - 439 + X = 782$

What is the value of X?

382	456	478	531

(2) A cube has a width of 5 m.

What is the volume of the cube?

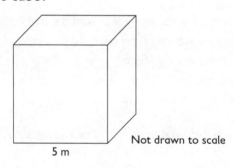

5 m

Not drawn to scale

125 cm^3	25 m^3	5 m^3	125 m^3

(3) What fraction of the names of the days of the week begin with the letter 'T'?

$\frac{2}{7}$	$\frac{5}{6}$	$\frac{1}{2}$	$\frac{1}{7}$

(4) How many more edges does a cube have than a sphere?

0	4	8	12

5 $7(J + 8) = 63$

What is the value of J?

9	2	7	1
⬭	⬭	⬭	⬭

6 It is −15°C in Iceland and 34°C in Qatar.

What is the difference in temperature between Iceland and Qatar?

49°C	−49°C	−15°C	−45°C
⬭	⬭	⬭	⬭

7 What is the range of this set of numbers?

71, 98, 43, 12, 39, 43, 43, 54, 71, 2, 12

43	96	98	58
⬭	⬭	⬭	⬭

8 This table shows the schedule followed by 2 buses.

How many minutes does it take Bus 1 to go from Stop B to Stop D?

Stop	Bus 1	Bus 2
A	08:34	08:45
B	08:39	08:49
C	08:45	08:56
D	08:52	09:03
E	08:59	09:10

16 minutes	11 minutes	3 minutes	13 minutes
⬭	⬭	⬭	⬭

9 Andy and Bella share £540 in the ratio 4:5.

How much more does Bella receive than Andy?

£0	£240	£60	£300
⬭	⬭	⬭	⬭

10 Ben has coloured balloons at his birthday party.

There are twice as many red balloons as blue balloons.

There are three times as many blue balloons as yellow balloons.

There are half as many pink balloons as yellow balloons.

If there are 12 pink balloons, how many red balloons are there?

72	12	84	144
⬭	⬭	⬭	⬭

Score: .... / 10

Test 2

You have 3 minutes to complete this test.

You have 5 questions to complete within the given time.

Use the diagram below to help you answer the questions in this test. Write the correct answer in the boxes provided (one digit per box).

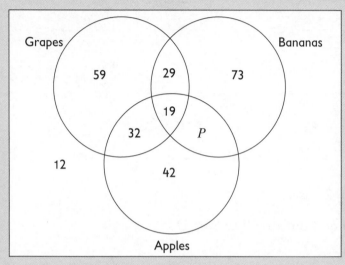

This Venn diagram shows the results of a survey about fruits liked by a group of students.

① How many students liked apples and grapes but not bananas?

② How many more students liked only apples than liked all 3 fruits?

③ How many students liked grapes?

④ What is the ratio of students who liked both grapes and apples but not bananas, to students who liked both bananas and grapes?

⑤ If 312 students took part in the survey, what is the value of *P*?

Score: .... / 5

Test 3

Write the correct answer in the boxes provided (one digit/sign per box).

EXAMPLE

Calculate 17 − 21

$\boxed{-}\ \boxed{4}$

---

(1) What value does the digit 9 represent in 213,931·53?

$\boxed{}\ \boxed{}\ \boxed{}$

(2) Linda and Greg share 345 apples in the ratio 7:8.

How many apples does Greg receive?

$\boxed{}\ \boxed{}\ \boxed{}$

(3) 7 sheep eat an average of 2·5 kg of grass each per day.

How much grass is eaten by the 7 sheep in 1 week?

$\boxed{}\ \boxed{}\ \boxed{}\ \cdot\ \boxed{}$ kg

(4) 750 students attend Daybreak School.

$\frac{1}{2}$ of the students at Daybreak School are boys.

$\frac{4}{5}$ of the girls at Daybreak School have brown hair.

How many girls at Daybreak School do not have brown hair?

$\boxed{}\ \boxed{}$

(5) The area of a square is 64 cm^2.

What is the perimeter of this square?

$\boxed{}\ \boxed{}$ cm

(6) How many more fifths are there in 25 than thirds in 39?

$\boxed{}$

(7) Helen has 32 pet fish. 12 of them are blue.

If Helen picks 1 fish at random, what is the probability that it is not blue? *Provide your answer as a fraction in its simplest form.*

$\boxed{}$ / $\boxed{}$

(8) Calculate 6 − ((7 × 9) − (8 × 7))

$\boxed{}\ \boxed{}$

Score: .... / 8

Test 4

You have 5 minutes to complete this test.

You have 10 questions to complete within the given time.

Circle the letter below the correct answer.

EXAMPLE

Round 32,134 to the nearest 100.

32,100	32,000	31,000	32,500
Ⓐ	B	C	D

---

1 Calculate $2\frac{1}{4} + 3\frac{1}{5}$

$5\frac{1}{2}$	$5\frac{9}{20}$	$5\frac{3}{4}$	$5\frac{4}{5}$
A	B	C	D

2 A fair die is rolled and a fair coin is tossed. What is the probablility of rolling a 3 <u>and</u> the coin landing on tails?

$\frac{1}{12}$	$\frac{1}{6}$	$\frac{1}{2}$	$\frac{1}{3}$
A	B	C	D

3 A function machine multiplies the input number by 7 and then divides by 2 to produce the output number.

If the output number is 42, what is the input number?

147	24	3	12
A	B	C	D

4 Every minute, a snail travels 2 cm north and 1·5 cm east.

How far east does the snail travel in 1 hour?

1·2 m	0.9 m	95 cm	30 cm
A	B	C	D

5 How many lines of symmetry does the letter **S** have?

0	1	2	3
A	B	C	D

(6) ABC is an equilateral triangle.
BCD is a straight line.

What is the value of f?

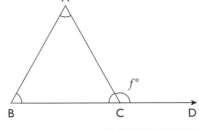

30°	60°	90°	120°
A	B	C	D

(7) Figure 1 is formed from a rectangle and 2 triangles.

What is the area of Figure 1?

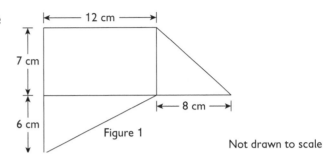

Figure 1

Not drawn to scale

114 cm²	84 cm²	148 cm²	120 cm²
A	B	C	D

(8) The cost of a holiday (C) in pounds can be calculated using the formula $C = 2(270W + 136)$ where W equals the number of weeks the holiday lasts for.

How much does it cost John to go on holiday for a fortnight?

£676	£3,916	£1,352	£7,832
A	B	C	D

(9) What is the median of these numbers?

9, 5, 3, 9, 1, 4, 7, 3, 9, 6

5·5	6	4	6·5
A	B	C	D

(10) Which word best describes angle A°?

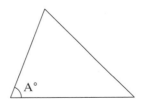

obtuse	acute	reflex	right angle
A	B	C	D

Score: .... / 10

9

Test 5

You have 5 minutes to complete this test.

You have 10 questions to complete within the given time.

Draw a line in the box below the correct answer.

EXAMPLE

Round 32,134 to the nearest 100.

| 32,100 | 32,000 | 31,000 | 32,500 |

---

① A lorry contains 724 red apples and 324 green apples. The apples are mixed together and put in boxes. Each box holds 25 apples.

How many boxes are needed to hold all the apples?

| 40 | 41 | 42 | 43 |

② How many multiples of 3 are greater than 212 but less than 228?

| 4 | 5 | 6 | 7 |

③ Bob wears a tie, a shirt and a jacket every day. He has 3 ties, 3 shirts and 4 jackets.

How many different combinations of tie, shirt and jacket can he choose from each day?

| 36 | 10 | 13 | 25 |

④ Figure A consists of 2 hexagons. The area of the small hexagon is three times smaller than the area of the large hexagon.

If the area of the large hexagon is 48 cm², what is the area of the shaded part?

Figure A

Not drawn to scale

| 16 cm² | 24 cm² | 32 cm² | 36 cm² |

(5) The average of 3 numbers is 17.

What is three times the sum of the 3 numbers?

| 51 | 153 | 102 | 17 |

(6) Following a discount of 30%, the price of a coat is £84.

What was the original price of the coat?

| £72·50 | £110 | £168 | £120 |

(7) A bag contains 7 red balls, 8 green balls and 5 blue balls.

If 1 ball is picked out of the bag at random, what is the probability that it is not blue?

$\frac{3}{4}$ $\qquad$ $\frac{5}{20}$ $\qquad$ $\frac{16}{20}$ $\qquad$ $\frac{8}{20}$

(8) Calculate the obtuse angle between the hour and the minute hand.

| 150° | 135° | 225° | 120·5° |

(9) Sam buys 5 pens for 25 p each and twice as many pencils for 40 p each.

If he pays with a £20 note, how much change does he receive?

| £16·75 | £14·75 | £4·75 | £5·25 |

(10) $7(Y + 4) = Y + Y + Y + 40$

What is the value of Y?

| 3 | 5 | 7 | 9 |

Score: .... / 10

11

Test 6

You have 3 minutes to complete this test.

You have 5 questions to complete within the given time.

Use the diagrams below to help you answer the questions in this test. Write the correct answer in the boxes provided (one digit per box).

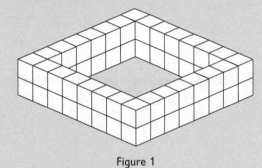

Figure 1

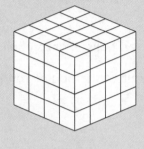

Figure 2

Not drawn to scale

Figures 1 and 2 are made from identical small cubes, each with a side length of 1 cm.

(1) What is the volume of Figure 2? ▢▢ cm³

(2) How many cubes are there in Figure 1? ▢▢

(3) What is the surface area of Figure 2? ▢▢ cm²

(4) Figure 2 is covered with a coat of red paint.

What fraction of the cubes in Figure 2 have exactly 2 faces painted red?

Write your answer as a fraction in its lowest terms.

$\frac{▢}{▢}$

(5) A larger version of Figure 1 is created using the same number of cubes, but each cube has a side length of 2 cm.

What is the volume of the new shape? ▢▢▢ cm³

Score: .... / 5

Test 7

Write the correct answer in the boxes provided (one digit per box).

EXAMPLE

How much longer is 2·7 m than 2·5 m? [2] [0] cm

---

(1) Theatre tickets are £4·50 for adults and half as much for children.

What is the total ticket cost for 2 adults and 2 children? £ [ ] [ ] · [ ] [ ]

(2) A dress is on sale with a 15% discount off the original price of £25. Amy buys 2 of these dresses.

How much does Amy spend? £ [ ] [ ] · [ ] [ ]

(3) $2A + 5P - (B - 3) = S$

If $A = 7$, $P = 5$ and $S = 35$, what is the value of B? [ ]

(4) A parallelogram has a length of 6 cm and a perpendicular height of 2·5 cm.

What is the area of the parallelogram? [ ] [ ] cm²

(5) 32,360 fans attended a rock concert, rounded to the nearest 20.

What is the largest possible number of fans who attended the concert? [ ] [ ] , [ ] [ ] [ ]

(6) Calculate 2^5 [ ] [ ]

(7) What is the internal angle of a regular hexagon? [ ] [ ] [ ]°

(8) What is the next number in this sequence?

45, 144, 244, 345, 447, ? [ ] [ ] [ ]

Score: .... / 8

13

Test 8

You have 5 minutes to complete this test.

You have 9 questions to complete within the given time.

Circle the letter below the correct answer.

Round 32,134 to the nearest 100.

32,100	32,000	31,000	32,500	32,200
Ⓐ	B	C	D	E

(1) What is 74% of 300?

222	210	74	144	95
A	B	C	D	E

(2) How many hours are there in August?

720	696	744	24	733
A	B	C	D	E

(3) A toy shop displays this sign:

Toys are priced at £4·80 each.

BUY 4 TOYS AND GET THE 5th ONE HALF PRICE

How much would 10 toys cost?

£48·00	£38·40	£43·20	£40·00	£31·15
A	B	C	D	E

(4) 400 books were sold in a bookshop in week 1.

During week 2, 10% fewer books were sold than in week 1.

In week 3, 10% more books were sold than in week 2.

How many books were bought in week 3?

400	384	360	320	396
A	B	C	D	E

5 The average speed of a train over 5 hours was 110 kph (kilometres per hour).

The average speed of the train for the first 3 hours was 90 kph.

What was the average speed of the train for the last 2 hours in kph?

280 kph	130 kph	120 kph	140 kph	110 kph
A	B	C	D	E

6 This table shows the number of books read per week by 4 children.

How many books do the 4 children read in 4 weeks?

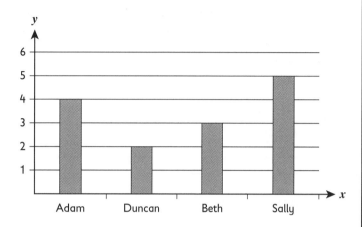

28	14	48	36	56
A	B	C	D	E

7 In a class of students, there are 18 boys and 13 girls. 9 of the students have brown hair and 14 of the students wear glasses.

What is the largest possible number of girls who have brown hair but do not wear glasses?

9	13	5	21	11
A	B	C	D	E

8 Tim is a salesman at a television company. Every month, he is paid a base salary of £750 and 25% commission on the value of each television he sells. In June, Tim sold 5 televisions with an average price of £400.

How much was Tim paid in June?

£500	£3,250	£750	£1,250	£1,800
A	B	C	D	E

9 Harry rode his motorcycle 150 km over 2 days.

He rode four times as far on the second day than the first day.

How much further did he ride on the second day?

120 km	30 km	90 km	110 km	25 km
A	B	C	D	E

Score: .... / 9

Test 9

You have 5 minutes to complete this test.

You have 10 questions to complete within the given time.

Draw a line in the box below the correct answer.

EXAMPLE

Round 32,134 to the nearest 100.

32,100	32,000	31,000	32,500
▭	▭	▭	▭

---

(1) 5 books cost the same as 3 pencils. 2 pens cost the same as 1 pencil. 3 rubbers cost the same as 1 pen.

How many rubbers cost the same as 5 books?

15	1	18	6
▭	▭	▭	▭

(2) Which number comes next in this sequence?

0, 7, 26, 63, ?

126	124	7	96
▭	▭	▭	▭

(3) Henry wishes to cover his garden with pieces of turf. Each piece of turf measures 25 cm by 20 cm. The measurements of the garden are shown below:

5 m

Henry's garden   4 m

Not drawn to scale

How many pieces of turf does Henry need to cover his whole garden?

500	20	200	400
▭	▭	▭	▭

(4) Calculate 586 × 79

56,294	46,294	46,284	47,294
▭	▭	▭	▭

(5) How many minutes are there in 1 day?

2,400 ⬭   60 ⬭   3,600 ⬭   1,440 ⬭

(6) Jane has a collection of 480 marbles.

$\frac{1}{3}$ of them are blue, $\frac{1}{8}$ of them are red and $\frac{1}{5}$ of them are yellow. The remainder are green.

How many green marbles does Jane have?

316 ⬭   240 ⬭   164 ⬭   220 ⬭

(7) Train A covers a distance of 120 km in 60 minutes. Train B covers the same distance in 120 minutes.

What is the average speed of the 2 trains in kph (kilometres per hour)?

120 kph ⬭   80 kph ⬭   60 kph ⬭   90 kph ⬭

(8) How many factors does the number 36 have?

6 ⬭   7 ⬭   8 ⬭   9 ⬭

(9) On the grid to the right, 1 unit represents 3 km.

Alex starts a journey at Point G.

He travels in a straight line to (1,2) and then in a straight line to (1,6).

How many kilometres does Alex cover?

6 km ⬭   12 km ⬭   15 km ⬭   18 km ⬭

(10) A faulty clock runs 120 seconds fast per hour.

If the clock currently shows the time 03:54, what time will it show in exactly 4 hours?

08:02 ⬭   07:54 ⬭   07:58 ⬭   11:54 ⬭

Score: .... / 10

Test 10

Use the clocks below to help you answer the questions in this test. Write the correct answer in the boxes provided (one digit per box).

NEW YORK
04:15

LONDON
10:15

HONG KONG
17:15

These clocks show the current time in 3 different parts of the world.

Write your answers in 24-hour clock format.

(1) How many hours ahead is the time in Hong Kong than the time in New York? ☐☐ hours

(2) When it is 16:52 in London, what time is it in New York? ☐☐ : ☐☐

(3) The time in Zurich is 1 hour ahead of the time in London.

If it is 14:21 in Hong Kong, what time is it in Zurich? ☐☐ : ☐☐

(4) Neil goes to bed at 22:00 in New York and sleeps for 8 hours.

What time is it in Hong Kong when he wakes up? ☐☐ : ☐☐

(5) The flight time from New York to Hong Kong is 15 hours.

If a flight leaves New York for Hong Kong at 07:10 local time, what time will it be in London when it lands? ☐☐ : ☐☐

Score: .... / 5

18

Test 11

You have 4 minutes to complete this test.

You have 8 questions to complete within the given time.

Write the correct answer in the boxes provided (one digit per box).

EXAMPLE

How much longer is 2·7 m than 2·5 m?

$\boxed{2}\boxed{0}$ cm

---

(1) A map is drawn on a scale of 1:250,000.

What is the actual distance represented by 2 cm on the map?

$\boxed{}$ km

(2) 1 angle in an isosceles triangle is 102°.

Write down the measurement of another angle in this triangle.

$\boxed{}\boxed{}$°

(3) 5,622 × 842 = 4,733,724

What is 4,733,724 ÷ 11,244?

$\boxed{}\boxed{}\boxed{}$

(4) Book A weighs 320 g, Book B weighs 453 g and Book C weighs 843 g.

What is the total weight of the 3 books?

$\boxed{}\cdot\boxed{}\boxed{}\boxed{}$ kg

(5) How many cubes with a 2 cm width can fit into a cube with an 8 cm width?

$\boxed{}\boxed{}$

(6) 175,000 people live in Town R. 45% of them are men and the rest are women. 50% of the women are married.

How many of the women in Town R are unmarried?

$\boxed{}\boxed{},\boxed{}\boxed{}\boxed{}$

(7) What is the time $4\frac{1}{6}$ hours before 02:07?
Use the 24-hour clock format.

$\boxed{}\boxed{}:\boxed{}\boxed{}$

(8) The numerator of a fraction is 12 less than the denominator. The fraction is equivalent to $\frac{1}{5}$.

What is the numerator of the fraction?

$\boxed{}$

Score: .... / 8

Test 12

You have 5 minutes to complete this test.

You have 9 questions to complete within the given time.

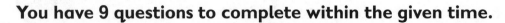

Circle the letter below the correct answer.

EXAMPLE

Round 32,134 to the nearest 100.

32,100	32,000	31,000	32,500
Ⓐ	B	C	D

---

(1) How many more factors does 48 have than 24?

8	2	10	6
A	B	C	D

(2) How much liquid is in the container to the right?

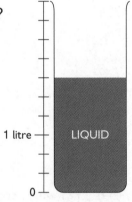

1 litre

LIQUID

0

1·33 litres	1·66 litres	2 litres	2·33 litres
A	B	C	D

(3) Calculate $2\frac{1}{3} - 1\frac{4}{5}$

$\frac{8}{15}$	$\frac{3}{5}$	$\frac{4}{15}$	$\frac{4}{5}$
A	B	C	D

(4) What is the next term in this sequence?

74, 68, 70, 64, 66, 60, ?

62	66	54	64
A	B	C	D

(5) Which equation correctly describes the relationship between A and B in the table below?

A	7	4	8
B	11	5	13

$B = A + 4$	$B = 2A - 3$	$B = A + 1$	$B = 3A - 11$
A	**B**	**C**	**D**

(6) The net below forms a cube when folded.

When folded, which face of the cube will not be adjacent to Face B?

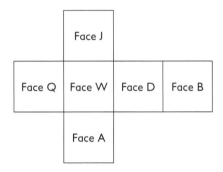

Face Q	Face J	Face A	Face W
A	**B**	**C**	**D**

(7) The distance between Town A and Town B is 3·46 km to 2 decimal places.

What is the maximum possible distance between Town A and Town B to the nearest metre?

3·464	3,465	3,464	3,455
A	**B**	**C**	**D**

(8) 4 camels eat 250 nuts per day each.

How many nuts do 8 camels eat in 2 weeks?

28,000	4,000	7,000	14,000
A	**B**	**C**	**D**

(9) Sam weighs 32·5 kg and Daniel is 10% lighter than Sam.

What is their mean weight, rounded to 2 decimal places?

30·875 kg	30·874 kg	30·87 kg	30·88 kg
A	**B**	**C**	**D**

Score: .... / 9

Test 13

You have 5 minutes to complete this test.

You have 10 questions to complete within the given time.

Draw a line in the box below the correct answer.

EXAMPLE

Round 32,134 to the nearest 100.

32,100	32,000	31,000	32,500
▭	⬭	⬭	⬭

(1) A total of 808 members attend a conference. The ratio of male to female members is 3:5.

How many more females attended the conference than males?

202	303	404	505
⬭	⬭	⬭	⬭

(2) TRE is an isosceles triangle. Angle T is 96°.

What is the size of angle R?

90°	84°	96°	42°
⬭	⬭	⬭	⬭

(3) 4 students took a test and their average score was 34.

2 of the students both scored 36.

1 of the students scored 40.

What did the final student score?

36	24	40	136
⬭	⬭	⬭	⬭

(4) There are 4 tomatoes, 6 oranges and 5 bananas in a bag.

Alicia picks out a tomato and does not replace it.

Alicia then picks out 1 more item at random.

What is the probability that this item is a banana?

$\frac{1}{3}$	$\frac{6}{14}$	$\frac{5}{14}$	$\frac{1}{2}$
⬭	⬭	⬭	⬭

5 How many different ways are there to arrange 3 books in a row on a shelf?

99 ⬭   3 ⬭   6 ⬭   12 ⬭

6 According to this train timetable, how long does it take to travel from Trovald to Provald if the 17:57 train is taken?

Brovald	17:32	18:45	20:20
Trovald	17:57	—	20:59
Krovald	18:14	19:30	—
Provald	18:34	19:50	21:44

30 minutes ⬭   37 minutes ⬭   46 minutes ⬭   52 minutes ⬭

7 4 of the internal angles in a pentagon are 92°, 45°, 110° and 136°.

What is the size of the 5th internal angle in this pentagon?

160° ⬭   157° ⬭   47° ⬭   132° ⬭

8 4 boxes and 3 drums cost £9·90.
3 boxes and 2 drums cost £7.

What is the cost of 1 box and 1 drum?

£2·90 ⬭   £1·70 ⬭   £1·45 ⬭   £1·20 ⬭

9 Subtract the smallest square number from the largest prime number from the list of numbers in the box below.

56, 45, 90, 100, 43, 18, 25, 96, 64, 17, 59

42 ⬭   18 ⬭   34 ⬭   27 ⬭

10 Figure 1 is made of identical cubes.
Each cube has a side length of 2 cm.

What is the volume of Figure 1?

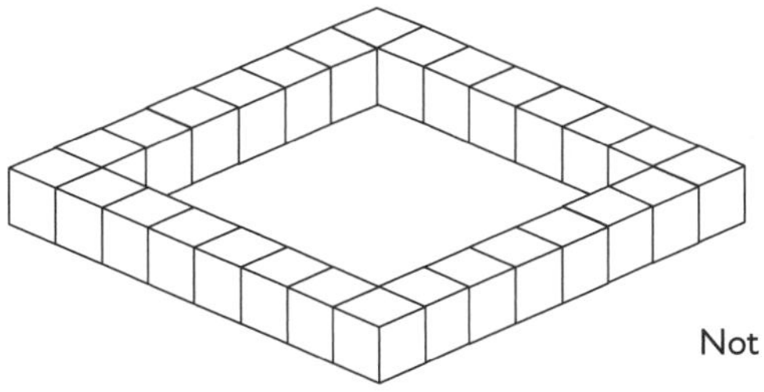

Not drawn to scale

Figure 1

224 cm³ ⬭   8 cm³ ⬭   32 cm³ ⬭   28 cm³ ⬭

Score: .... / 10

23

Test 14

You have 3 minutes to complete this test.

You have 5 questions to complete within the given time.

Use the table below to help you answer the questions in this test. Write the correct answer in the boxes provided (one digit/sign per box).

City	Temperature (°C)
Paris	3
Tokyo	7
Moscow	−7
Atlanta	−2
Cairo	12
Oslo	−9
Cape Town	25
Algiers	?

This table shows the daytime temperature in 8 cities on 1 day in December.

(1) What is the range of the temperatures, excluding Algiers and Moscow?

(2) How many degrees warmer was it in Cairo than in Moscow?

(3) What was the mean temperature of Moscow, Oslo and Atlanta?

(4) The night-time temperature in Cape Town on that day was 40% less than the daytime temperature.

What was the night-time temperature in Cape Town on that day?

(5) The mode temperature is 12°C.

What is the temperature in Algiers?

Score: .... / 5

24

Test 15

You have 4 minutes to complete this test.

You have 8 questions to complete within the given time.

Write the correct answer in the boxes provided (one digit per box).

EXAMPLE

How much longer is 2·7 m than 2·5 m? | 2 | 0 | cm

(**1**) 7 friends each drink 2 cans of cola per day.

How many cans do they drink in total in July? ☐☐☐

(**2**) 3 angles in a pentagon are 45°, 67° and 111°.

What is the sum of the other 2 angles in the pentagon? ☐☐☐ °

(**3**) 4 eggs are needed to bake a cake that serves 8.

How many eggs are needed to bake a cake that serves 60? ☐☐

(**4**) A sequence is derived by tripling the previous term and then subtracting 3.

If the 5th term in the sequence is 42, what is the 2nd term? ☐

(**5**) 7 children take 3 hours to paint a board.

How long will it take 21 children to paint the same board? ☐☐ minutes

(**6**) P is a whole number that is a multiple of 6 and satisfies the inequality $P > 122$.

What is the smallest possible value of P? ☐☐☐

(**7**) The internal angle of an equilateral triangle is $(5x)°$.

What is the value of x? ☐☐

(**8**) Paul completed a game in 35 seconds. Henry took 5 more seconds than Paul to complete the game. Max completed the game 8 seconds slower than Henry.

What was their mean game completion time? ☐☐ seconds

Score: .... / 8

Test 16

You have **5 minutes** to complete this test.

You have **9 questions** to complete within the given time.

Circle the letter below the correct answer.

EXAMPLE

Round 32,134 to the nearest 100.

32,100	32,000	31,000	32,500	32,200
Ⓐ	B	C	D	E

1 Fabian and Kate both start writing sentences at 9 a.m. Fabian writes 64 sentences per hour and Kate writes 72 sentences per hour. They both stop writing sentences at 12:30 p.m.

How many sentences do they write in total?

252	38	224	476	422
A	B	C	D	E

2 $A = B(4 \times 0) \div (9 + C)$

What is the value of A?

0	1	2	3	4
A	B	C	D	E

3 Every 7 minutes, a special cell splits itself into 2. These cells will also split into 2 every 7 minutes.

If there is 1 cell at 2:00 p.m., how many cells will there be at 2:21 p.m.?

4	8	14	16	6
A	B	C	D	E

4 6 years ago, the combined age of 3 boys was 27.

What will the combined age of the 3 boys be next year?

45	38	33	30	48
A	B	C	D	E

5 $K = (4 \times B^2)$

$K = \frac{1}{3} \times (600 \div P)$

$P = 2$

Calculate $K + P - B$

97	220	102	92	95
A	**B**	**C**	**D**	**E**

6 Triangle B is made up of congruent smaller triangles, each with an area of 2·75 cm².

What is three times the area of Triangle B?

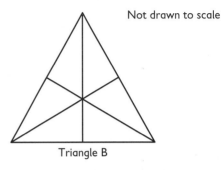

Not drawn to scale

Triangle B

49·5 cm²	2·75 cm²	32 cm²	16·5 cm²	18·5 cm²
A	**B**	**C**	**D**	**E**

7 A farmer places a stake at each end of his field and then every 8 metres in a straight line between the 2 ends.

If the distance between the 2 ends is 768 metres, how many stakes does the farmer use?

96	95	97	98	99
A	**B**	**C**	**D**	**E**

8 1 Rog is worth 8 Rigs. 2 Rigs are worth 9 Regs.

How many Regs are worth 4 Rogs?

32	144	81	64	24
A	**B**	**C**	**D**	**E**

9 Figure G is made from squares, each with an area of 2·25 cm².

What is the perimeter of Figure G?

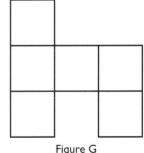

Not drawn to scale

Figure G

19 cm	14 cm	12 cm	21 cm	32 cm
A	**B**	**C**	**D**	**E**

Score: .... / 9

Test 17

You have 5 minutes to complete this test.

You have 10 questions to complete within the given time.

Draw a line in the box below the correct answer.

EXAMPLE

Round 32,134 to the nearest 100.

32,100	32,000	31,000	32,500
▭	▭	▭	▭

① Divide 9,555 by 35.

269	273	282	251
▭	▭	▭	▭

② $\frac{X}{4} = 44$

What is the value of X?

88	11	132	176
▭	▭	▭	▭

③ How many cubes of side 2 cm can be fitted into a cuboid measuring 6 cm by 2 cm by 4 cm?

6	24	48	384
▭	▭	▭	▭

④ Calculate the value of angle Y.

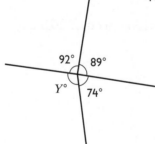

Not drawn to scale

84°	207°	105°	111°
▭	▭	▭	▭

5 A box contains an equal number of five-pence and two-pence coins with a total value of £2·24.

How many five-pence coins are there in the box?

20	50	16	32
☐	☐	☐	☐

6 The coordinates of Point P are (7, 5). Point D is a reflection of Point P in the y-axis.

What are the coordinates of Point D?

(–7, 5)	(7, 5)	(7, –5)	(–7, –5)
☐	☐	☐	☐

7 An ant travels 20 cm per minute.

What is the ant's speed in metres/hour?

120 metres/hour	200 metres/hour	1,200 metres/hour	12 metres/hour
☐	☐	☐	☐

8 The letters D, R and Y each represent a single-digit number in the sum below.

What is the value of Y?

$$\begin{array}{ccc} & 3 & R & 5 \\ + & Y & 8 & D \\ \hline & 6 & 3 & 2 \end{array}$$

2	7	4	3
☐	☐	☐	☐

9 The length of a rectangle is G and the width is $G - 7$.

Which expression represents the perimeter of the rectangle?

$2G - 7$	$4G + 14$	$4G - 14$	$4G - 7$
☐	☐	☐	☐

10 A triangle has 3 different internal angles that are all square numbers.

What is the largest angle in the triangle?

81°	121°	144°	100°
☐	☐	☐	☐

Score: .... / 10

Test 18

You have 3 minutes to complete this test.

You have 5 questions to complete within the given time.

Use the number cards below to help you answer the questions in this test. Write the correct answer in the boxes provided (one digit per box).

7		1		4	
	8		9		6

1. What is the largest number that can be made by using 3 of the number cards in any order?

2. Subtract the largest number that can be made by using 5 of the number cards in any order from the smallest number that can be made by using all 6 of the number cards in any order.

3. What is the product of the values on the largest and smallest number cards?

4. What is the smallest odd number that can be made by using 3 of the number cards in any order?

5. A number card is picked at random.

   What is the probability that it is a prime number?

Score: .... / 5

30

Test 19

You have 4 minutes to complete this test.

You have 8 questions to complete within the given time.

Write the correct answer in the boxes provided (one digit per box).

EXAMPLE

How much longer is 2·7 m than 2·5 m? **2** **0** cm

---

(1) Calculate $5^3 - 3^4$ ☐☐

(2) What percentage of 7 kg is 2,800 g? ☐☐ %

(3) A circle has a radius of 3·25 cm.

What is 8 times the diameter of the circle? ☐·☐☐ m

(4) 8 out of 10 lions in a zoo are female.

There are 40 lions in the zoo.

What is the probability that a lion picked at random is male? ☐ / ☐

(5) 20% of X is 100. What is 10% of X? ☐☐

(6) $7(y + 8) = 91$

What is the value of y? ☐

(7) The ratio of apples to oranges in a shop is 1:1·25.

If there are 12 apples in the shop, how many oranges are there? ☐☐

(8) Set G consists of all the factors of 24.

Set P consists of all the factors of 30.

How many numbers are in set P but not in set G? ☐

Score: .... / 8

Test 20

You have 5 minutes to complete this test.

You have 9 questions to complete within the given time.

Circle the letter below the correct answer.

EXAMPLE

Round 32,134 to the nearest 100.

32,100	32,000	31,000	32,500
Ⓐ	B	C	D

---

(1) How many hours are there between 9 a.m. on 28th May and 2 a.m. on 3rd June?

135	137	122	120
A	B	C	D

(2) 7 copies of a book cost £42·42.

How many copies of the book can be bought with £18·16?

1	2	3	4
A	B	C	D

(3) What is the range of these numbers?

9·999, 9·989, 9·889, 9·898, 9·995

0·11	0·1	0·01	0·101
A	B	C	D

(4) Beth wishes to catch Train 2. She arrives at the station at 14:37. Train 2 is 17 minutes late.

For how long must Beth wait at the station?

	Train 1	Train 2	Train 3
Departure Time	14:34	14:59	15:24

22 minutes	17 minutes	28 minutes	39 minutes
A	B	C	D

(5) A bag contains $\frac{3}{8}$ red balls, $\frac{2}{5}$ blue balls and the rest are green.

There are 18 green balls in the bag.

How many red balls are in the bag?

80	32	15	30
A	**B**	**C**	**D**

(6) 3 cogs are turning together.

Cog 1 turns 4 times when Cog 2 turns 9 times.

Cog 3 turns 6 times when Cog 1 turns 8 times.

How many times does Cog 3 turn when Cog 2 turns 27 times?

8	12	9	21
A	**B**	**C**	**D**

(7) A 3 litre jug is $\frac{3}{4}$ full. It is used to fill 4 cups that each hold 125 ml.

How much liquid is left in the jug?

1·75 litres	2·4 litres	0·6 litres	1·4 litres
A	**B**	**C**	**D**

(8) There are an equal number of boys and girls on a bus.

At the first stop, 7 boys get off.

At the second stop, 1 boy gets on.

There are now twice as many girls than boys on the bus.

How many children were on the bus to begin with?

12	18	24	30
A	**B**	**C**	**D**

(9) I place 6 squares side by side in a straight line, to form a rectangle.

Each square has a perimeter of 20 cm.

What is the perimeter of the rectangle?

120 cm	70 cm	60 cm	80 cm
A	**B**	**C**	**D**

Score: .... / 9

Test 21

You have 5 minutes to complete this test.

You have 10 questions to complete within the given time.

Draw a line in the box below the correct answer.

EXAMPLE

Round 32,134 to the nearest 100.

32,100	32,000	31,000	32,500
▭̲	▭	▭	▭

---

(1) Calculate 12·5642 – 7·849

5·4793	4·7512	4·7152	20·4132
▭	▭	▭	▭

(2) A sequence of numbers is made by adding a constant each time.

The 2nd term in the sequence is 12 and the 6th term is 36.

What is the 8th term in the sequence?

42	50	48	52
▭	▭	▭	▭

(3) The product of 2 different prime numbers is 143.

What is the smaller prime number?

7	11	13	5
▭	▭	▭	▭

(4) What is the difference between the smallest and second largest four-digit number that can be made using the digits on the cards below, once each?

7	5	9	3

4,374	6,174	3,579	6,156
▭	▭	▭	▭

(5) Which number is closest in value to 7·3?

$7\frac{1}{5}$ ⬭

$7\frac{8}{20}$ ⬭

7·271 ⬭

$7\frac{1}{2}$ ⬭

(6) Fred and Yosef share £2·56 between them. Yosef receives 18 p more than Fred.

How much does Fred receive?

£2·38 ⬭

£1·37 ⬭

£1·52 ⬭

£1·19 ⬭

(7) A storage box holds 10 identical shirts. It weighs 3·456 kg.

If the storage box weighs 346 g, what is the weight of 3 shirts?

933 g ⬭

3·11 kg ⬭

346 g ⬭

311 g ⬭

(8) Sanika is 7th in a queue and 13th from the back.

How many people are in the queue?

19 ⬭

20 ⬭

21 ⬭

22 ⬭

(9) The area of Triangle B is 48 cm².

Triangle C has the same base as Triangle B but double the height.

What is the height of Triangle C?

Triangle B

6 cm

Not drawn to scale

16 cm ⬭

8 cm ⬭

24 cm ⬭

32 cm ⬭

(10) What whole number multiplied by 37 gives the smallest possible four-digit number?

27 ⬭

28 ⬭

29 ⬭

30 ⬭

Score: .... / 10

35

Test 22

You have 3 minutes to complete this test.

You have 5 questions to complete within the given time.

Use the diagram below to help you answer the questions in this test. Write the correct answer in the boxes provided (one digit per box) or draw a line in the box below the correct answer.

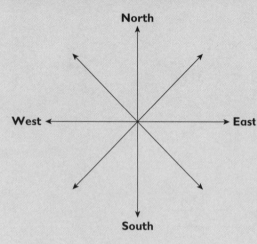

(1) What is the smaller angle between north and southeast? ☐☐☐°

(2) What is the bearing of west from northwest? ☐☐☐°

(3) John faces east and turns anticlockwise to face northwest.

Jim faces east and turns clockwise to face northwest.

How much greater is the angle that Jim turns? ☐☐°

(4) A flag points south and then turns 225° clockwise.

What fraction of a full turn has the flag made?

Write your answer as a fraction in its lowest terms.

☐
—
☐

(5) Arthur faces north and then turns 540° clockwise.

What direction is Arthur now facing?

north   southwest   east   south

⬭   ⬭   ⬭   ⬭

Score: .... / 5

Test 23

You have 4 minutes to complete this test.

You have 8 questions to complete within the given time.

Write the correct answer in the boxes provided (one digit per box).

EXAMPLE

How much longer is 2·7 m than 2·5 m?

⟦2⟧⟦0⟧ cm

---

(1) 3 consecutive odd numbers add up to 39.

What is the largest number?

⟦ ⟧⟦ ⟧

(2) $0·456 < X < 0·464$

What is the value of X to 2 decimal places?

⟦ ⟧·⟦ ⟧⟦ ⟧

(3) The perimeter of a rectangle is 26 cm and the length is 9 cm.

What is the area of the rectangle?

⟦ ⟧⟦ ⟧ cm²

(4) $A = 20$, $B = 5$, $C = 2$

What is $4A$ in terms of B?

⟦ ⟧⟦ ⟧ B

(5) Calculate 7,024 – 6,678

⟦ ⟧⟦ ⟧⟦ ⟧

(6) R, T and Q are the 3 largest prime numbers less than 20.

What is the sum of R, T and Q?

⟦ ⟧⟦ ⟧

(7) Express 0·625 as a fraction in its simplest form.

⟦ ⟧
⟦ ⟧

(8) A sculpture is made from a cube and a cuboid attached together.

The cube has sides of 3 cm and the cuboid has dimensions
3 cm × 4 cm × 5·5 cm.

What is the volume of the sculpture?

⟦ ⟧⟦ ⟧ cm³

Score: .... / 8

Test 24

You have 5 minutes to complete this test.

You have 9 questions to complete within the given time.

Circle the letter below the correct answer.

EXAMPLE

Round 32,134 to the nearest 100.

32,100	32,000	31,000	32,500	32,200
Ⓐ	B	C	D	E

---

(1) What is 1 m² in cm²?

1 cm²	100 cm²	10,000 cm²	100,000 cm²	1,000,000 cm²
A	B	C	D	E

(2) Cylinder A has a height of 7 cm.

The circular face has an area of 2·75 cm².

What is the volume of Cylinder A?

Not drawn to scale

Cylinder A

7 cm³	15 cm³	18 cm³	19·25 cm²	19·25 cm³
A	B	C	D	E

(3) There are 80 questions in a test. Mark answered 75% of the questions and got 60% of these questions correct.

How many questions did Mark get correct?

75	60	42	36	55
A	B	C	D	E

(4) $x^2 = 3^2 + 4^2$

What is the value of x?

5	4	16	25	36
A	B	C	D	E

5 What is the value of R?

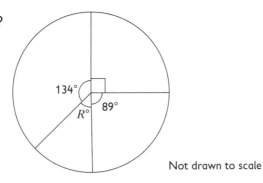

Not drawn to scale

58°	47°	90°	39°	42°
A	**B**	**C**	**D**	**E**

6 In a beehive, 750 bees hatch in 5 days.

Each day, 10 more bees hatch than the day before.

How many bees hatch on the 4th day?

150	134	160	168	122
A	**B**	**C**	**D**	**E**

7 There are 17 silver fish in a pond. 9 of them are large and the rest are small.

The small fish each have 200 scales and the large fish each have twice as many scales as the small fish.

How many scales do all the fish have in total?

4,400	16,000	3,600	2,500	5,200
A	**B**	**C**	**D**	**E**

8 A white cube has a volume of 64 cm³.

Ginny covers one half of 1 face of the cube with black paint.

What fraction of the cube's surface area is now white?

$\frac{1}{2}$	$\frac{11}{12}$	$\frac{1}{6}$	$\frac{2}{6}$	$\frac{1}{5}$
A	**B**	**C**	**D**	**E**

9 HRQ is a three-digit number.

The first digit is $\frac{1}{4}$ of the last digit.

The second digit is 8 more than the first digit.

What is the number?

862	164	153	194	234
A	**B**	**C**	**D**	**E**

Score: .... / 9

Test 25

You have 5 minutes to complete this test.

You have 10 questions to complete within the given time.

Draw a line in the box below the correct answer.

EXAMPLE

Round 32,134 to the nearest 100.

| 32,100 | 32,000 | 31,000 | 32,500 |

① 2 parts squash are mixed with 6 parts water to create 2 litres of drink.

How much of the drink is water?

| 1·5 litres | 0·8 litres | 500 ml | 750 ml |

② The area of the white circle is $\frac{2}{9}$ of the area of the black circle.

The area of the white circle is 90 cm².

What is the area of the black circle?

Not drawn to scale

| 20 cm² | 360 cm² | 200 cm² | 405 cm² |

③ 7 carrots, 8 cucumbers and 12 potatoes cost £3·65.

10 carrots, 8 cucumbers and 12 potatoes cost £3·86.

What is the cost of 4 cucumbers and 6 potatoes?

| £2·45 | £0·21 | £1·58 | £3·16 |

④ How many square numbers are there between 401 and 999?

| 9 | 10 | 11 | 12 |

40

(5) My watch is slow and loses 2 minutes every half an hour.

If it shows the correct time at 2 p.m., what time will it show when the correct time is 5:30 p.m.?

5:23 p.m.	5:16 p.m.	5:30 p.m.	5:46 p.m.
☐	☐	☐	☐

(6) Katie buys 12 apples for 60 p each.

Katie sells half of the apples for £1·20 each and sells the other half for £1·80 each.

How much profit does Katie make?

£18	£10·80	£10	£7·20
☐	☐	☐	☐

(7) Which amount can be made using exactly 4 coins?

78 p	86 p	93 p	64 p
☐	☐	☐	☐

(8) I throw a fair die.

What is the probability that it lands on a prime number?

$\frac{1}{6}$	$\frac{1}{3}$	$\frac{1}{2}$	$\frac{5}{6}$
☐	☐	☐	☐

(9) Rob, Sarah and Peter took a test. There were 48 marks available.

Rob scored $\frac{42}{48}$. Sarah scored half the marks. Peter scored $\frac{5}{6}$ of the marks.

How many marks did they score in total?

74	96	84	106
☐	☐	☐	☐

(10) How many lines of symmetry does this shape have?

0	1	2	3
☐	☐	☐	☐

Score: .... / 10

Test 26

Use the diagram below to help you answer the questions in this test. Write the correct answer in the boxes provided (one digit per box).

Figure 1

Not drawn to scale

Figure 1 consists of 9 identical squares, each with side length of 2·5 cm.

(1) What is the area of Figure 1? ☐☐·☐☐ cm²

(2) What is the perimeter of Figure 1? ☐☐ cm

(3) What is the order of rotational symmetry of Figure 1? ☐

(4) A tick is drawn in 1 of the squares in Figure 1.

What is the probability that the ticked square lies on the edge of Figure 1? ☐/☐

(5) How many different squares are formed by the lines in Figure 1? ☐☐

Score: .... / 5

Test 27

You have 4 minutes to complete this test.

You have 7 questions to complete within the given time.

Write the correct answer in the boxes provided (one digit/sign per box).

EXAMPLE

Calculate 17 − 21

[−][4]

---

(1) Ben and Gina eat at a restaurant. Their food bill comes to £53·30. A 10% service charge is added to this amount.

What is the total amount paid by Ben and Gina?

£ [ ][ ] · [ ][ ]

(2) How many minutes are there in 3 days?

[ ] , [ ][ ][ ] minutes

(3) The maximum temperature in Siberia in December is −3°C.

The temperature range in Siberia in December is 26°C.

What is the lowest temperature in December in Siberia?

[ ][ ][ ]°C

(4) Kelly eats $\frac{1}{4}$ of a pizza and gives away $\frac{1}{2}$ of the remainder.

What fraction of the pizza remains?

$\dfrac{[\ ]}{[\ ]}$

(5) How many edges does a hexagonal prism have?

[ ][ ]

(6) $\frac{1}{3}(Y) + \frac{2}{3}(Y) = 7$

What is the value of $2Y$?

[ ][ ]

(7) What fraction of 2 days is 2 hours?

Write your answer as a fraction in its lowest terms.

$\dfrac{[\ ]}{[\ ][\ ]}$

Score: .... / 7

43

Test 28

You have 5 minutes to complete this test.

You have 10 questions to complete within the given time.

Circle the letter below the correct answer.

EXAMPLE

Round 32,134 to the nearest 100.

32,100	32,000	31,000	32,500
(A)	B	C	D

(1) What is the order of rotational symmetry of this shape?

0	1	2	5
A	B	C	D

(2) Express $1\frac{5}{8}$ as a decimal.

1·615	1·585	1·625	1·675
A	B	C	D

(3) The bearing of F from B is 73°.

What is the bearing of B from F?

253°	107°	287°	197°
A	B	C	D

(4) The ratio of red frogs to green frogs in a pond is 7:4. There are 44 frogs in total.

What is the probability that a frog chosen at random is red?

$\frac{4}{11}$	$\frac{4}{7}$	$\frac{28}{42}$	$\frac{7}{11}$
A	B	C	D

(5) How many different combinations of coins can equal 7 p?

6	7	8	9
A	B	C	D

(6) 8 cows eat 3 kg of grass in 2 hours.

How much grass do 24 cows eat in 1 hour?

9 kg	4·5 kg	5 kg	6 kg
A	B	C	D

(7) Alan bakes muffins and places them on to plates. Each plate holds 7 muffins. Alan has 4 muffins left over.

Which of the following could be the total number of muffins baked by Alan?

53	86	35	100
A	B	C	D

(8) 7 oranges, 5 strawberries and 4 apples cost 82 p altogether.

Apples cost twice as much as strawberries. Apples cost half as much as oranges.

How much does a strawberry cost?

8 p	1 p	4 p	2 p
A	B	C	D

(9) Shape B is an equilateral triangle.

What fraction of Shape B is shaded?

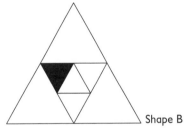

Shape B

$\frac{1}{18}$	$\frac{1}{8}$	$\frac{1}{16}$	$\frac{1}{15}$
A	B	C	D

(10) The students in class A stand in a circle. They are evenly spaced from each other.

The 4th student is opposite the 14th student.

How many students are there in the circle?

28	26	22	20
A	B	C	D

Score: .... / 10

45

Test 29

You have 5 minutes to complete this test.

You have 10 questions to complete within the given time.

Draw a line in the box below the correct answer.

EXAMPLE

Round 32,134 to the nearest 100.

32,100	32,000	31,000	32,500
⬡	▭	▭	▭

(1) Hannah needs to catch a train at 4:47 p.m. She leaves home at 3:36 p.m. and it takes her 37 minutes to arrive at the train station.

For how long must Hannah wait at the train station before her train departs?

34 minutes	37 minutes	71 minutes	36 minutes
▭	▭	▭	▭

(2) 7 cows each produce 3 litres of milk per day. This milk is put into bottles that hold 250 ml each.

How many bottles of milk do the cows produce each week?

21	84	588	1,088
▭	▭	▭	▭

(3) $\frac{1}{4}$ of a number is four times $\frac{1}{6}$ of 84.

What is the number?

56	14	224	168
▭	▭	▭	▭

(4) Roy collects cards. He notices that whether he divides his cards into piles of 4, 6 or 8, he has no cards left over.

What is the smallest number of cards that Roy could own?

16	24	32	48
▭	▭	▭	▭

(5) Which of these numbers is closest to 4?

3·7232	4·2458	3·7284	4·2368
▭	▭	▭	▭

(6) Shape B consists of 7 identical circles placed inside a hexagon.

The area of each circle is 2·5 cm².

The area of the hexagon is 10% greater than the total area of the circles.

What is the area of the hexagon?

Not drawn to scale

Shape B

2·5 cm²	19·25 cm²	17·5 cm²	15 cm²
⬭	⬭	⬭	⬭

(7) 751 × 1,500 = 1,126,500

What is 751 × 750?

1,126,500	844,875	563,250	281,625
⬭	⬭	⬭	⬭

(8) A menu at a restaurant is shown below:

Item	Price
Meal 1	£8·65
Meal 2	£5·99
Meal 3	£7·54
Drink	£1·25

Gail orders Meal 1 and a drink. A 10% service charge is added to her bill.

How much does Gail pay?

£11	£9·90	£10·50	£10·89
⬭	⬭	⬭	⬭

(9) Roman pays £2·20 for the first 20 minutes of his internet usage and then £0·20 for every minute thereafter.

If Roman uses the internet for 42 minutes, how much does he pay?

£2·20	£4·40	£6·60	£8·80
⬭	⬭	⬭	⬭

(10) Natasha has an equal number of 2 p, 5 p and 20 p coins. She has a total of £1·89.

What is the total number of 2 p and 5 p coins that Natasha has?

14	7	2	21
⬭	⬭	⬭	⬭

Score: .... / 10

Test 30

Use the grid below to help you answer the questions in this test. Write the correct answer in the boxes provided (one digit per box) or draw a line in the box below the correct answer.

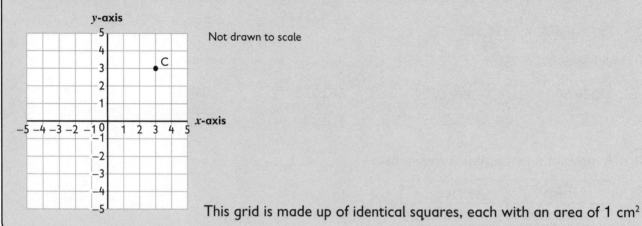

Not drawn to scale

This grid is made up of identical squares, each with an area of 1 cm²

1. Point D is the reflection of point C in the *x*-axis.

   What are the coordinates of point D?

   (3, −3)   (−3, 3)   (−3, −3)   (3, 3)

2. Point F is the reflection of point D in the *y*-axis.

   What are the coordinates of point F?

   (3, −3)   (−3, 3)   (−3, −3)   (3, 3)

3. Points C, F, D and B are the 4 vertices of a square.

   What are the coordinates of point B?

   (3, −3)   (−3, 3)   (−3, −3)   (3, 3)

4. The coordinates of point X are (0, −3). Points X, C and B form a triangle.

   What is the area of this triangle?   ☐☐ cm²

5. What is the area of the triangle XFC?   ☐ cm²

Score: .... / 5

48

Test 31

Write the correct answer in the boxes provided (one digit per box).

EXAMPLE

How much longer is 2·7 m than 2·5 m?

$\boxed{2}\boxed{0}$ cm

---

(1) A band sells tickets for a concert. They have sold 80% of the 1,500 tickets so far. The band withholds 10% of the remaining tickets for friends and family.

How many tickets do they withhold?

$\boxed{}\boxed{}$

(2) A restaurant has 32 tables. Half the tables can seat 6 people, a quarter can seat 7 people and the rest can seat 8 people.

What is the maximum number of diners that can be seated in the restaurant?

$\boxed{}\boxed{}\boxed{}$

(3) The mean of $7F$, $3F$ and $2F$ is 24.

What is the value of F?

$\boxed{}$

(4) A sequence is formed by adding X to the previous term. The 1st term in the sequence is 2 and the 5th term is 30.

What is the 3rd term in the sequence?

$\boxed{}\boxed{}$

(5) $\frac{2}{7}$ of the children in a group have blue eyes. There are 14 children with blue eyes in the group.

How many children are there in the group?

$\boxed{}\boxed{}$

(6) The ratio of success to failure of experiments in a science laboratory is 7:3.

If the laboratory performs 100 experiments, how many more successes will there be than failures?

$\boxed{}\boxed{}$

(7) $A + B = C$

$C - 8 = A$

$AB = 56$

What is $C + B - A$?

$\boxed{}\boxed{}$

Score: .... / 7

49

Test 32

Circle the letter below the correct answer.

EXAMPLE

Round 32,134 to the nearest 100.

32,100	32,000	31,000	32,500	32,200
(A)	B	C	D	E

1. Ali has a piece of ribbon measuring 2 m 43 cm. He cuts it into strips, each measuring 3 cm.

   How many strips does Ali have?

79	84	102	21	81
A	B	C	D	E

2. X is the cost of $\frac{1}{5}$ of a theatre ticket.

   Which expression shows the value of 5 theatre tickets?

$5X$	X	$25X$	$15X$	$2X$
A	B	C	D	E

3. The average of 4 consecutive even numbers is 35.

   What is the largest number?

37	36	39	38	42
A	B	C	D	E

4. Harry is three times older than Amir.

   Amir is $(X - 4)$ years old.

   How old is Harry?

$3X - 12$	$X - 4$	$3X - 4$	$X - 12$	$X + 5$
A	B	C	D	E

(5) Calculate $\frac{9}{1} + \frac{1}{9} + \frac{9}{1}$

$18\frac{1}{9}$	$\frac{9}{1}$	$9\frac{1}{9}$	18	16
A	B	C	D	E

(6) $\frac{5}{6} + T < 1$

Which of the following could be the value of T?

$\frac{1}{2}$	$\frac{1}{4}$	$\frac{1}{6}$	$\frac{1}{3}$	$\frac{1}{8}$
A	B	C	D	E

(7) Shape R is a regular pentagon. AB is a straight line.

What is the value of V?

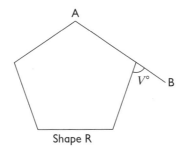

Shape R   Not drawn to scale

72°	108°	90°	112°	84°
A	B	C	D	E

(8) $Y + Y + Y = 15$

$X + X - Y = 45$

$Z + X + Y = 60$

What is the value of Z?

5	30	15	20	25
A	B	C	D	E

(9) Calculate $\frac{1}{4} \times \frac{1}{3}$

$\frac{3}{4}$	$\frac{1}{12}$	$\frac{4}{3}$	$\frac{12}{1}$	$\frac{7}{4}$
A	B	C	D	E

Score: .... / 9

Test 33

You have 5 minutes to complete this test.

You have 10 questions to complete within the given time.

Draw a line in the box below the correct answer.

EXAMPLE

Round 32,134 to the nearest 100.

32,100	32,000	31,000	32,500
▭	▭	▭	▭

---

(1) 5 friends rent a car for a weekend. The rental cost is £45 plus £1·50 for each kilometre driven. They drive 51 kilometres in total. They decide to split the cost equally between them.

How much does each friend pay?

£121·50	£76·50	£15·30	£24·30
▭	▭	▭	▭

(2) 2 whole numbers between 20 and 30 multiply together to give 525.

What is the smaller number?

21	22	23	24
▭	▭	▭	▭

(3) Tom can read 6 books in 8 days.

How many books can Tom read in 20 days?

12	15	18	24
▭	▭	▭	▭

(4) If $x - 7 = 21$ and $3y + 8 = 32$, what is $2x + y$?

28	36	64	44
▭	▭	▭	▭

(5) An equilateral triangle has a perimeter of 1,035 cm.

What is the total length of 2 sides of the triangle?

345 cm	900 cm	690 cm	103 cm
▭	▭	▭	▭

6 The table below shows the birth dates of 5 friends born in 2008.

Who is the second youngest?

	Birthday
Linda	16th August
Amy	11th May
Ayesha	11th June
Kate	7th August
Alice	4th January

Amy ⬭   Ayesha ⬭   Kate ⬭   Linda ⬭

7 Esther is 5 years more than double Amelia's age.

If Amelia is $(F - 1)$ years old, how old is Esther?

$2F - 4$ ⬭ $3 + 2F$ ⬭ $2F + 4$ ⬭ $5F - 5$ ⬭

8 Simon completes a game in $3\frac{1}{3}$ hours. Henry completes it in $2\frac{1}{5}$ hours and James completes it in $2\frac{5}{6}$ hours.

What is their total completion time in minutes?

450 ⬭   482 ⬭   502 ⬭   543 ⬭

9 The function $A\rightarrow B$ means multiply A by B and then subtract B.

Using this rule, what is $7\rightarrow8$?

56 ⬭   49 ⬭   64 ⬭   48 ⬭

10 Figure 1 consists of 8 identical cubes.

The volume of Figure 1 is 1,000 cm³.

What is the surface area of Figure 1?

Not drawn to scale

Figure 1

450 cm² ⬭   25 cm² ⬭   1,200 cm² ⬭   750 cm² ⬭   900 cm² ⬭

Test 34

You have 3 minutes to complete this test.

You have 5 questions to complete within the given time.

Use the shapes below to help you answer the questions in this test. Write the correct answer in the boxes provided (one digit per box).

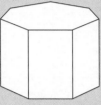

Figure 1

Figure 2

Figure 3

Not drawn to scale

1. Figure 1 is made from heptagons and rectangles.

   Each heptagon has an area of 25·21 cm².

   Each rectangle has a width of 2 cm and a length of 3 cm.

   What is the surface area of Figure 1?

   ⬜⬜·⬜⬜ cm²

2. How many more edges than faces does Figure 2 have?

   ⬜⬜

3. What is the volume of Figure 1?

   ⬜⬜·⬜⬜ cm³

4. What is the total number of faces in Figures 1, 2 and 3?

   ⬜⬜

5. What is the total number of edges in Figures 1, 2 and 3?

   ⬜⬜

Score: .... / 5

54

Test 35

Write the correct answer in the boxes provided (one digit per box).

EXAMPLE

How much longer is 2·7 m than 2·5 m?   [2][0] cm

---

(1) Olivia buys a magazine for 30% off its original price of £13.

How much did Olivia pay?   £[ ].[ ][ ]

(2) A triangle has a base of G cm and height of U cm.

If GU is 46 cm², what is the area of the triangle?   [ ][ ] cm²

(3) What is the lowest common multiple of 16 and 14?   [ ][ ][ ]

(4) Express $\frac{17}{20}$ as a decimal.   [ ].[ ][ ]

(5) What is the product of 22 and 21?   [ ][ ][ ]

(6) A pie chart is used to show the favourite colour of a group of 280 children.

70 children chose red and 150 chose blue.

What is the angle of the pie chart sector that represents red?   [ ][ ]°

(7) Calculate $\frac{3}{4} \times \frac{4}{5}$

Write your answer as a fraction in its lowest terms. $\frac{[\ ]}{[\ ]}$

(8) A rectangular field measures 25 m by 30 m.

$\frac{2}{3}$ of the surface of the field is covered by grass.

What is the surface area of the field that is not covered in grass?   [ ][ ][ ] m²

Score: .... / 8

55

Test 36

You have 5 minutes to complete this test.

You have 10 questions to complete within the given time.

Circle the letter below the correct answer.

EXAMPLE

Round 32,134 to the nearest 100.

32,100	32,000	31,000	32,500
Ⓐ	B	C	D

---

(1) AC is a straight line.

What is the value of B?

Not drawn to scale

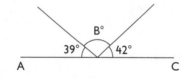

100°	74°	99°	89°
A	B	C	D

(2) What is the next number in this sequence?

1,343, 1,327, 1,312, 1,298, ?

1,286	1,287	1,285	1,284
A	B	C	D

(3) On average, Keith sleeps for $7\frac{1}{2}$ hours per day.

For how many hours does Keith sleep in December?

210	$210\frac{1}{2}$	$232\frac{1}{2}$	232
A	B	C	D

(4) $P < 8$

Which of the following could be the value of $9P + 7$?

61	79	88	97
A	B	C	D

(5) The length of a rectangle is 54 cm and its perimeter is 110 cm.

What is the area of the rectangle?

108 cm²	54 cm²	27 cm²	5400 cm²
A	B	C	D

(6) The 3 angles in a scalene triangle are 54°, $W°$ and $U°$.

Which of the following cannot be the value of $W°$?

90°	1°	63°	55°
A	B	C	D

(7) Calculate 10,000 × 0·002 × 7

200	140	1,400	14,000
A	B	C	D

(8) The ratio of cold days to hot days in 2015 in Spain was 1:4.

How many hot days were there in Spain in 2015?

292	120	73	219
A	B	C	D

(9) The internal angles in a quadrilateral are $T°$, $2T°$, $2T°$ and $4T°$.

What is the largest angle in the quadrilateral?

40°	80°	100°	160°
A	B	C	D

(10) Which word best describes this shape?

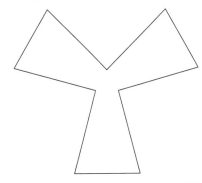

obtuse	quadrilateral	nonagon	reflexive
A	B	C	D

Score: .... / 10

Test 37

You have 5 minutes to complete this test.

You have 10 questions to complete within the given time.

Draw a line in the box below the correct answer.

EXAMPLE

Round 32,134 to the nearest 100.

| 32,100 | 32,000 | 31,000 | 32,500 |

---

(1) What is the product of 543 and 39?

| 21,717 | 21,177 | 21,171 | 21,117 |

(2) If 21st August is a Sunday, what day is 7th September of the same year?

| Tuesday | Wednesday | Thursday | Friday |

(3) Liam faces southwest and then turns 225° anticlockwise.

Which direction does Liam now face?

| northeast | northwest | west | north |

(4) Figure 1 is formed from a square with side length of 4·5 cm and an equilateral triangle.

What is the perimeter of Figure 1?

4·5 cm

Not drawn to scale

Figure 1

| 13·5 cm | 22 cm | 18 cm | 22·5 cm |

5 27,575 ants live in an area of 25 m².

What is the population density of the ants?
(Population density = ants/m²)

| 1,104 | 1,100 | 1,103 | 1,105 |

6 The digits 4, 7, 8 and 4 are randomly arranged to form a four-digit number.

What is the probability that the number ends in 4?

$\frac{1}{4}$ $\frac{1}{2}$ $\frac{3}{4}$ $\frac{7}{8}$

7 Which number is greater than $6\frac{5}{6}$ but less than $6\frac{7}{8}$?

6·83 6·86 6·89 6·92

8 Rhombus D has an internal angle of 73°.

Which of these is also an internal angle of Rhombus D?

214° 103° 107° 74°

9 This diagram shows a sphere inside a cube.

The sphere touches each face of the cube.

The sphere has a radius of 5 cm.

What is the volume of the cube?

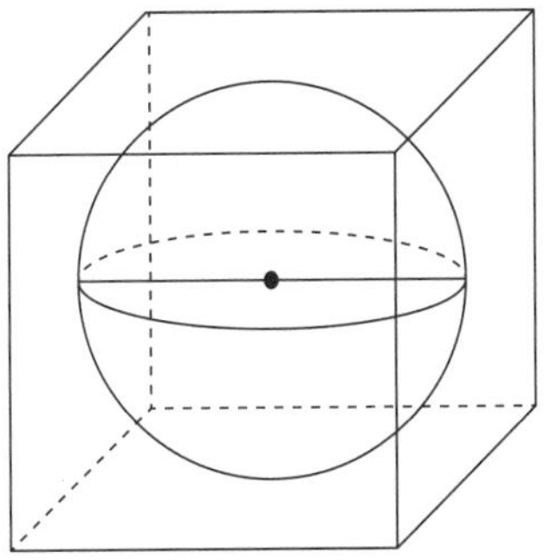

Not drawn to scale

1,000 cm³ 25 cm³ 125 cm³ 575 cm³

10 Triangle B is equilateral with sides of 5 cm.

How many times can Triangle B fit inside a regular hexagon of side 10 cm?

4 20 24 18

Score: .... / 10

Test 38

You have 3 minutes to complete this test.

You have 5 questions to complete within the given time.

Use the diagrams below to help you answer the questions in this test. Write the correct answer in the boxes provided (one digit/sign per box).

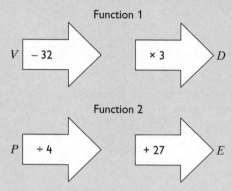

Function 1

V -32 $\times 3$ D

Function 2

P $\div 4$ $+27$ E

The diagrams above show 2 functions.

---

(1) What is the value of V if $D = 18$?

(2) What is the value of P if $E = 39$?

(3) What is the mean of D and E when $V = 33$ and $P = 8$?

(4) If the input of Function 1 is 17, what is the output?

(5) If the output of Function 2 is 27, what is the input?

Score: .... / 5

Test 39

You have 4 minutes to complete this test.

You have 8 questions to complete within the given time.

Write the correct answer in the boxes provided (one digit per box).

How much longer is 2·7 m than 2·5 m?   ☐2☐ ☐0☐ cm

---

1 Lampposts are placed at the beginning and end of a street and every 7 metres along it. The street is 343 metres long.

How many lampposts are there on the street?   ☐ ☐

2 Calculate $3 \times \frac{4}{5}$

Write your answer as a decimal.   ☐ . ☐

3 What is the next number in this sequence?

73, 71, 67, 61, 59, 53, ?   ☐ ☐

4 Bill is twice as tall as Tim. Tim is three times taller than Kim.

How many times taller is Bill than Kim?   ☐

5 $4B + C = 20$, $B + C = 20$

What is the value of B?   ☐

6 What is the remainder when 676 is divided by 12?   ☐

7 What is the time $6\frac{6}{8}$ hours before 14:21?   ☐ ☐ : ☐ ☐

8 How many faces does a triangular prism have?   ☐

Score: .... / 8

Test 40

You have 5 minutes to complete this test.

You have 10 questions to complete within the given time.

Circle the letter below the correct answer.

EXAMPLE

Round 32,134 to the nearest 100.

32,100	32,000	31,000	32,500	32,200
Ⓐ	B	C	D	E

(1) Which of the following is not equal to $\frac{4}{5}$?

0·8	$\frac{24}{30}$	80%	$\frac{32}{42}$	$\frac{44}{55}$
A	B	C	D	E

(2) Marc takes 4 tests. His scores are 56, 22, 0 and 81.

What is Marc's mean score?

53	41	39·75	38·5	32
A	B	C	D	E

(3) Each of a lorry's wheels has a circumference of 100 cm.

How many times does each wheel turn if the lorry travels 72 km?

100,000	65,000	7,200	70,200	72,000
A	B	C	D	E

(4) Figure A is formed from identical regular hexagons.

The area of each hexagon is 36 cm².

The height of each hexagon is 6 cm.

What is the perimeter of Figure A?

Not drawn to scale

Figure A

64 cm	32 cm	60 cm	54 cm	50 cm
A	B	C	D	E

5 A map is drawn on the scale 1:500,000,000.

What is the actual measurement of a distance of 1 mm on the map?

500 km	500,000 cm	50,000,000 m	5,000 km	5,000 cm
A	**B**	**C**	**D**	**E**

6 A ramp is placed against the wall of a building.

The angle between the ramp and the flat ground is 23°.

What is the angle between the ramp and the wall?

90°	45°	33°	27°	67°
A	**B**	**C**	**D**	**E**

7 There are 7 dozen nuts in a bag.

6 monkeys each remove 7 nuts from the bag.

What fraction of the nuts remain?

$\frac{1}{4}$	$\frac{1}{2}$	$\frac{41}{84}$	$\frac{3}{8}$	$\frac{1}{5}$
A	**B**	**C**	**D**	**E**

8 14 divided by Y gives a remainder of 2.

How many different integer values of Y are possible?

3	6	2	4	5
A	**B**	**C**	**D**	**E**

9 What is the product of the number of edges and the number of faces in Figure 1?

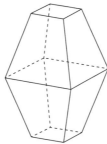

Figure 1

180	150	200	190	170
A	**B**	**C**	**D**	**E**

10 Calculate $0{\cdot}8 + \frac{3}{8}$

1·075	1·175	$\frac{7}{8}$	$\frac{1}{375}$	1·21
A	**B**	**C**	**D**	**E**

Score: .... / 10

Test 41

You have **5 minutes** to complete this test.

You have **10 questions** to complete within the given time.

Draw a line in the box below the correct answer.

EXAMPLE

Round 32,134 to the nearest 100.

32,100	32,000	31,000	32,500
⊏══⊐	⊏⊐	⊏⊐	⊏⊐

① What is the surface area of this cube?

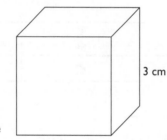

3 cm

Not drawn to scale

54 cm²	12 cm²	9 cm²	72 cm²
⊏⊐	⊏⊐	⊏⊐	⊏⊐

② The population of Town A is 550,000, rounded to the nearest 1,000.

$\frac{1}{2}$ of the population of Town A have black hair.

What is the smallest possible number of people in Town A with black hair?

549,500	274,750	275,500	275,000
⊏⊐	⊏⊐	⊏⊐	⊏⊐

③ Jill cycles for $2\frac{1}{4}$ hours and then rests for $\frac{1}{2}$ hour before cycling for another $1\frac{1}{4}$ hours.

She covers 140 km in total.

What is Jill's average speed for the whole journey in kph (kilometres per hour)?

31·1 kph	40 kph	35 kph	50 kph
⊏⊐	⊏⊐	⊏⊐	⊏⊐

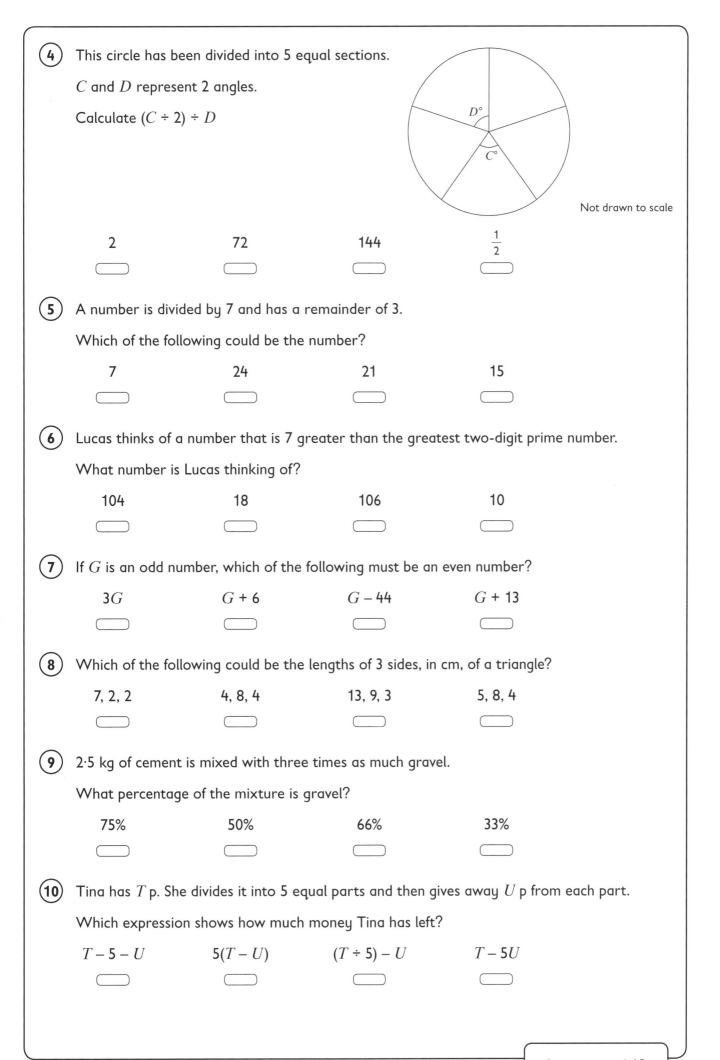

4 This circle has been divided into 5 equal sections.

C and D represent 2 angles.

Calculate $(C \div 2) \div D$

$D°$

$C°$

Not drawn to scale

| 2 | 72 | 144 | $\frac{1}{2}$ |

5 A number is divided by 7 and has a remainder of 3.

Which of the following could be the number?

| 7 | 24 | 21 | 15 |

6 Lucas thinks of a number that is 7 greater than the greatest two-digit prime number.

What number is Lucas thinking of?

| 104 | 18 | 106 | 10 |

7 If G is an odd number, which of the following must be an even number?

| $3G$ | $G + 6$ | $G - 44$ | $G + 13$ |

8 Which of the following could be the lengths of 3 sides, in cm, of a triangle?

| 7, 2, 2 | 4, 8, 4 | 13, 9, 3 | 5, 8, 4 |

9 2·5 kg of cement is mixed with three times as much gravel.

What percentage of the mixture is gravel?

| 75% | 50% | 66% | 33% |

10 Tina has T p. She divides it into 5 equal parts and then gives away U p from each part.

Which expression shows how much money Tina has left?

| $T - 5 - U$ | $5(T - U)$ | $(T \div 5) - U$ | $T - 5U$ |

Score: .... / 10

Test 42

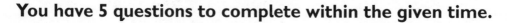

You have 3 minutes to complete this test.

You have 5 questions to complete within the given time.

Use the images below to help you answer the questions in this test. Write the correct answer in the boxes provided (one digit per box).

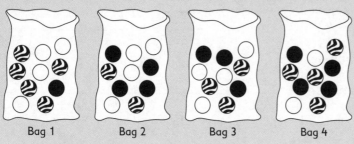

Bag 1   Bag 2   Bag 3   Bag 4

The diagrams to the left show the number of white, black and striped marbles in 4 bags.

(1) 1 marble is picked from Bag 2 at random.

What is the probability that it is black?

Write your answer as a fraction in its lowest terms.

(2) A white marble is picked out of Bag 3 but not replaced. Another marble is then picked out of Bag 3 at random.

What is the probability that this marble is striped?

Write your answer as a fraction in its lowest terms.

(3) If the contents of Bag 1 and Bag 4 are mixed and then 1 marble is picked at random, what is the probability that it is white?

Write your answer as a fraction in its lowest terms.

(4) What is the probability that a black marble is picked at random out of Bag 2 and a striped marble is picked at random out of Bag 4?

Write your answer as a fraction in its lowest terms.

(5) What is the probability that a white marble is picked at random from Bag 3 (not replaced) and then another white marble is picked at random from the same bag?

Write your answer as a fraction in its lowest terms.

Score: .... / 5

Test 43

Write the correct answer in the boxes provided (one digit per box).

EXAMPLE

How much longer is 2·7 m than 2·5 m?

| 2 | 0 | cm |

1. What percentage of 60 is 90?

☐☐☐ %

2. It takes Hilary 30 seconds to run around a track.

How many times can she run around the track in $\frac{5}{6}$ of an hour?

☐☐☐

3. How many eighths are there in 63?

☐☐☐

4. A milk bottle holds $\frac{3}{4}$ litres of milk.

Greg has 7 milk bottles, each $\frac{1}{2}$ full.

How much milk is in Greg's bottles?

☐ · ☐☐☐ litres

5. $2Y < 30$

What is the largest possible integer value of Y?

☐☐

6. I draw lines to divide a circle into 15 equal segments.

What is the angle closest to the centre of the circle of 1 segment?

☐☐ °

7. $30 + F = 32$, $30F = B$

What is the value of B?

☐☐

8. Fred runs 12 kilometres in 40 minutes.

What is Fred's speed in kph (kilometres per hour)?

☐☐ kph

Score: .... / 8

Test 44

You have 5 minutes to complete this test.

You have 9 questions to complete within the given time.

Circle the letter below the correct answer.

EXAMPLE

Round 32,134 to the nearest 100.

32,100	32,000	31,000	32,500
Ⓐ	B	C	D

(1) Jon runs 15 times faster than Paul.

How far can Paul run in the time it takes Jon to run 4·5 km?

300 m	1·3 km	750 m	1·5 km
A	B	C	D

(2) $Y✪ = 6Y + 6$

What is the value of the function $8✪ - 2✪$?

24	18	36	54
A	B	C	D

(3) The time in Delhi is 8 hours ahead of the time in London.

The time in Los Angeles is 9 hours behind the time in London.

If it is 21:00 in Los Angeles, what time is it in Delhi?

14:00	11:00	03:00	16:00
A	B	C	D

(4) The point (8, 9) is reflected in the x-axis and then reflected in the y-axis to make Point D.

What are the coordinates of Point D?

(8, 9)	(−8, 9)	(−8, −9)	(8, −9)
A	B	C	D

5 $b^3 - c^2 = y$

$b < c < 10$

If y equals 39, what is the value of c?

25	64	49	5
A	**B**	**C**	**D**

6 Tom collects sticks. His stick collection is shown below.

How many more sticks does Tom need to have **47** sticks in total?

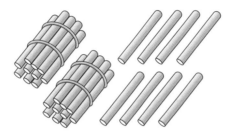

18	19	75	23
A	**B**	**C**	**D**

7 Flora picks at random an integer greater than 17 but less than 41?

What is the probability that Flora picks an even number?

$\frac{11}{22}$	$\frac{12}{23}$	$\frac{1}{2}$	$\frac{13}{24}$
A	**B**	**C**	**D**

8 $2(\frac{1}{2}(16(X))) = 64$

What is the value of X?

2	4	6	8
A	**B**	**C**	**D**

9 The morning temperature in Moscow is shown on this thermometer.

In the afternoon, the temperature increased by a dozen degrees.

It then decreased by **17** degrees at night.

What was the temperature at night?

7°	10°	−10°	−12°
A	**B**	**C**	**D**

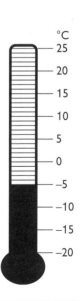

Score: .... / 9

Test 45

You have 3 minutes to complete this test.

You have 5 questions to complete within the given time.

Use the shapes below to help you answer the questions in this test. Write the correct answer in the boxes provided (one digit per box).

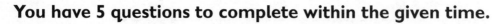

Figure 1   Figure 2   Figure 3   Figure 4

---

(1) Figure 1 is an isosceles triangle.

1 angle in the triangle is 117°.

What is three times the sum of the other 2 angles?

☐☐☐°

(2) Figure 3 is a regular octagon.

What is the sum of the internal angles of Figure 3?

☐,☐☐☐°

(3) Figure 4 is a regular hexagon and Figure 2 is a regular pentagon.

How much greater is an exterior angle from Figure 2 than an exterior angle from Figure 4?

☐☐°

(4) What is the order of rotational symmetry of Figure 3?

☐

(5) How many more lines of symmetry does Figure 4 have than Figure 1?

☐

Score: .... / 5

70

Answers

Key abbreviations: °C: degrees centigrade, b: base, cm: centimetre, d.p.: decimal place, g: gram, h: height, kg: kilogram, km: kilometre, kph: kilometres per hour, l: length, LCM: lowest common multiple, m: metre, mins: minutes, ml: millilitre, mm: millimetre, R: remainder, w: width

Test 1

Q1 **478**

743 − 439 = 304 so X = 782 − 304 = 478

Q2 **125 m³**

Volume = width × length × height = 5 m × 5 m × 5 m = 125 m³

Q3 $\frac{2}{7}$

7 days in a week; 2 of them begin with T (Tuesday and Thursday) so $\frac{2}{7}$

Q4 **12**

Cube has 12 edges; sphere has 0 edges so 12 − 0 = 12

Q5 **1**

$(J + 8) = 63 \div 7$; $J + 8 = 9$ so $J = 1$

Q6 **49°C**

−15°C → 0°C is 15°C; 0°C → 34°C is 34°C;
15°C + 34°C = 49°C

Q7 **96**

Range = largest number − smallest number
= 98 − 2 = 96

Q8 **13 minutes**

08:39 → 08:52 is 13 minutes

Q9 **£60**

9 equal parts; 1 part = £540 ÷ 9 = £60
Bella receives 5 × £60 = £300
Andy receives 4 × £60 = £240
£300 − £240 = £60

Q10 **144**

Work backwards: 12 pink → 24 yellow → 72 blue → 144 red

Test 2

Q1 **32**

Q2 **23**

42 students liked only apples; 19 students liked all 3 fruits
42 − 19 = 23

Q3 **139**

Students who liked grapes = 59 + 29 + 19 + 32 = 139

Q4 **2:3**

Students who liked both grapes and apples but not bananas = 32
Students who liked both bananas and grapes
= 29 + 19 = 48
32:48 = 2:3

Q5 **46**

P = 312 − 59 − 29 − 19 − 32 − 73 − 42 − 12 = 46

Test 3

Q1 **900**

9 is in the hundreds column

Q2 **184**

7:8 means 15 parts in total
345 ÷ 15 = 23; 23 × 8 = 184

Q3 **122·5**

7 × 2·5 × 7 = 122·5 kg

Q4 **75**

$\frac{1}{2}$ of 750 = 375 boys so there are also 375 girls
$\frac{4}{5}$ of 375 = 300 girls with brown hair
So girls without brown hair = 375 − 300 = 75

Q5 **32**

8 cm × 8 cm = 64 cm² so side length is 8 cm
Perimeter = 8 cm × 4 = 32 cm

Q6 **8**

Fifths in 25 = 25 ÷ $\frac{1}{5}$ = 25 × 5 = 125
Thirds in 39 = 39 ÷ $\frac{1}{3}$ = 39 × 3 = 117
125 − 117 = 8

Q7 $\frac{5}{8}$

Number of non-blue fish = 32 − 12 = 20
Probability of picking non-blue fish = $\frac{20}{32} = \frac{5}{8}$

Q8 **−1**

6 − ((7 × 9) − (8 × 7)) = 6 − (63 − 56) = 6 − 7 = −1

Test 4

Q1 **B**

$2\frac{1}{4} + 3\frac{1}{5} = 2\frac{5}{20} + 3\frac{4}{20} = 5\frac{9}{20}$

Q2 **A**

Probability of throwing a 3 = $\frac{1}{6}$
Probability of tossing a coin on tails = $\frac{1}{2}$
Probability of both = $\frac{1}{6} \times \frac{1}{2} = \frac{1}{12}$

Q3 **D**

Work backwards: 42 × 2 = 84
84 ÷ 7 = 12

Q4 **B**

60 minutes in 1 hour so 1·5 cm × 60 = 90 cm = 0·9 m

Q5 **A**

The letter **S** has no lines of symmetry.

Q6 **D**

ABC is equilateral so Angle ACB = 180° ÷ 3 = 60°
Angle ACD = 180° − Angle ACB = 180° − 60° = 120°

Q7 **C**

Divide into 3 parts:
Area of rectangle = 12 cm × 7 cm = 84 cm²
Area of triangle 1 = b × h × $\frac{1}{2}$ = 6 cm × 12 cm × $\frac{1}{2}$ = 36 cm²
Area of triangle 2 = b × h × $\frac{1}{2}$ = 8 cm × 7 cm × $\frac{1}{2}$ = 28 cm²
So total area = 84 cm² + 36 cm² + 28 cm² = 148 cm²

Q8 **C**

Holiday length = 2 weeks so C = 2((£270 × 2) + £136) = £1,352

Test 4 answers continue on next page

Q9 **A**

In order: 1, 3, 3, 4, 5, 6, 7, 9, 9, 9

Median = average of 2 numbers in the middle =

$(5 + 6) \div 2 = 11 \div 2 = 5 \cdot 5$

Q10 **B**

Angle A is less than 90° so it is acute

Test 5

Q1 **42**

$724 + 324 = 1{,}048$; $1{,}048 \div 25 = 41 \cdot 92$

So we need to round up to 42 boxes (as we cannot have 41·92 boxes)

Q2 **5**

213, 216, 219, 222, 225

Q3 **36**

Multiply the possibilities together → $3 \times 3 \times 4 = 36$

Q4 **32 cm²**

Area of small hexagon = $48 \div 3 = 16$ so shaded area = $48 - 16 = 32$

Q5 **153**

Average = 17 so sum = $17 \times 3 = 51$

Three times the sum = $51 \times 3 = 153$

Q6 **£120**

70% = £84 so 10% = £84 ÷ 7 = £12

So 100% = £12 × 10 = £120

Q7 $\frac{3}{4}$

Total balls = 20

Probability not blue = $\frac{15}{20} = \frac{3}{4}$

Q8 **135°**

Clock divided into twelve sections; each section is $360° \div 12 = 30°$

Hour hand is halfway between 10 and 11 so $30° \div 2 = 15°$

$30° + 30° + 30° + 30° + 15° = 135°$

Q9 **£14·75**

$5 \times £0 \cdot 25 = £1 \cdot 25$; $10 \times £0 \cdot 40 = £4$; $£1 \cdot 25 + £4 = £5 \cdot 25$;

$£20 - £5 \cdot 25 = £14 \cdot 75$

Q10 **3**

$7Y + 28 = 3Y + 40$; $7Y - 3Y = 40 - 28$; $4Y = 12$; $Y = 3$

Test 6

Q1 **64**

Each cube has a volume of 1 cm × 1 cm × 1 cm = 1 cm³

Figure 2 consists of 64 cubes so volume = 64 cm³

Q2 **56**

Q3 **96**

Surface area of 1 face = 4 cm × 4 cm = 16 cm²

6 faces in total so 6 × 16 cm² = 96 cm²

Q4 $\frac{3}{8}$

Total number of cubes = 64

Number of cubes with exactly 2 faces painted red = 24

$\frac{24}{64} = \frac{3}{8}$

Q5 **448**

Volume of 1 cube = 2 cm × 2 cm × 2 cm = 8 cm³

56 cubes in total so volume of the new shape = 56 × 8 cm³ = 448 cm³

Test 7

Q1 **13·50**

Child ticket = £4·50 ÷ 2 = £2·25

so (£4·50 × 2) + (£2·25 × 2) = £9 + £4·50 = £13·50

Q2 **42·50**

15% of £25 = £3·75 so she pays £21·25 per dress

So for 2 dresses: £21·25 × 2 = £42·50

Q3 **7**

$2(7) + 5(5) - (B - 3) = 35$ so $B - 3 = 4$ so $B = 7$

Q4 **15**

Area = length × height = 6 cm × 2·5 cm = 15 cm²

Q5 **32,369**

32,370 would be rounded up to 32,380 to nearest 20

Q6 **32**

$2^5 = 2 \times 2 \times 2 \times 2 \times 2 = 32$

Q7 **120**

Sum of angles in a hexagon = 720°

$720° \div 6 = 120°$

Q8 **550**

Sequence is +99 +100 +101 +102 so next term is +103

Test 8

Q1 **A**

74% of 100 = 74 so 74% of 300 = 74 × 3 = 222

Q2 **C**

24 hours in 1 day; 31 days in August so 24 × 31 = 744 hours

Q3 **C**

If 10 toys are bought, 2 are half-price so 9 toys are paid for £4·80 × 9 = £43·20

Q4 **E**

10% of 400 = 40 so week 2 sales = 400 − 40 = 360

10% of 360 = 36 so week 3 sales = 360 + 36 = 396

Q5 **D**

Distance = speed × time = 110 × 5 = 550 = total distance covered

Distance covered in first 3 hours = 90 × 3 = 270 km

So distance covered in last 2 hours = 550 − 270 = 280 km

Speed = distance/time = 280 ÷ 2 = 140 kph

Q6 **E**

Books read in 1 week = 4 + 2 + 3 + 5 = 14

Books read in 4 weeks = 14 × 4 = 56

Q7 **A**

Assume all students with brown hair are girls so 9 girls with brown hair.

Assume all students with glasses are boys so 0 girls with glasses.

So 9 − 0 = 9

Q8 **D**

Pay = £750 + 0·25 × (5 × £400) = £750 + £500 = £1,250

Q9 **C**

Assume first day he rode X km so second day he rode $4X$ km

$4X + X = 150$ so $5X = 150$ so $X = 30$

$4X - X = 120 - 30 = 90$ km

Test 9

Q1 **18**

Cost of 1 pen = cost of 3 rubbers so cost of 6 rubbers = cost of 1 pencil so cost of 18 rubbers = cost of 3 pencils

Since cost of 3 pencils = cost of 5 books then cost of 18 rubbers = cost of 5 books

Q2 **124**

Sequence is sequential cube numbers minus 1

Q3 **400**

Total garden area = 500 × 400 = 200,000 cm²

Area of 1 piece of turf = 25 × 20 = 500 cm²

Number of pieces required = 200,000 ÷ 500 = 400

Q4 **46,294**

Long multiplication

Q5 **1,440**

1 day = 24 hours; 1 hour = 60 minutes so 60 × 24 = 1,440

Q6 **164**

Blue is 480 ÷ 3 = 160

Red is 480 ÷ 8 = 60

Yellow is 480 ÷ 5 = 96

Green is 480 − 160 − 60 − 96 = 164

Q7 **90 kph**

Speed of Train A = 120 ÷ 1 = 120 kph

Speed of Train B = 120 ÷ 2 = 60 kph

Average speed = (120 + 60) ÷ 2 = 90 kph

Q8 **9**

1, 36, 2, 18, 3, 12, 4, 9, 6

Q9 **18 km**

Total units covered = 6; 1 unit = 3 km; 6 units = 18 km

Q10 **08:02**

Clock adds extra 2 minutes per hour so 8 minutes over 4 hours

4 hours 8 minutes after 03:54 is 08:02

Test 10

Q1 **13**

04:15 to 17:15 is 13 hours

Q2 **10:52**

New York is 6 hours behind London so 6 hours behind 16:52 is 10:52

Q3 **08:21**

London is 7 hours behind Hong Kong so 7 hours behind 14:21 is 07:21

Zurich is 1 hour ahead of London so 1 hour ahead of 07:21 is 08:21

Q4 **19:00**

Neil wakes up at 06:00 in New York

13 hours after 06:00 is 19:00

Q5 **04:10**

15 hours after 07:10 is 22:10 so this is the New York time when flight lands

6 hours after 22:10 is 04:10 so this is the London time when flight lands

Test 11

Q1 **5**

2 cm is equivalent to 500,000 cm

500,000 cm = 5,000 m = 5 km

Q2 **39**

Other 2 angles must be equal as triangle is isosceles

so (180° − 102°) ÷ 2 = 39°

Q3 **421**

11,244 = 2 × 5,622 so 4,733,724 ÷ 11,244 = 842 ÷ 2 = 421

Q4 **1·616**

320 g + 453 g + 843 g = 1,616 g = 1·616 kg

Q5 **64**

8 cm ÷ 2 cm = 4 cm so 4 × 4 × 4 = 64

Q6 **48,125**

55% × 175,000 = 96,250 women

50% × 96,250 = 48,125

Q7 **21:57**

$4\frac{1}{6}$ hours = 4 hours 10 minutes so 21:57

Q8 **3**

$\frac{1}{5} = \frac{3}{15}$

15 − 3 = 12

Test 12

Q1 **B**

Factors of 48: 1, 48, 2, 24, 3, 16, 4, 12, 6, 8

Factors of 24: 1, 24, 2, 12, 3, 8, 4, 6

10 − 8 = 2

Q2 **C**

3 divisions represents 1 litre so 6 divisions represents 2 litres

Q3 **A**

$2\frac{1}{3} - 1\frac{4}{5} = \frac{7}{3} - \frac{9}{5} = \frac{35}{15} - \frac{27}{15} = \frac{8}{15}$

Q4 **A**

The rule for the sequence is −6 +2 −6 +2 −6… so next term is +2 = 62

Q5 **B**

Substitute the values for A and B into each equation to find the correct one.

Q6 **D**

When folded, Face W will be opposite Face B.

Q7 **C**

3·46 km (2 d.p.) could be a maximum of 3·464 km = 3,464 metres

Q8 **A**

4 camels eat 1,000 nuts per day so 8 camels eat 2,000 nuts per day

2 weeks = 14 days so 2,000 × 14 = 28,000

Q9 **D**

10% of 32·5 kg = 3·25 kg so Daniel's weight = 32·5 kg − 3·25 kg = 29·25 kg

Mean weight = (29·25 kg + 32·5 kg) ÷ 2 = 61·75 kg ÷ 2 = 30·875 = 30·88 kg (2 d.p.)

Test 13

Q1 **202**

3 + 5 = 8 parts; 808 ÷ 8 = 101 so number of males = 3 × 101 = 303

Number of females = 5 × 101 = 505 so the difference is 505 − 303 = 202

Q2 **42°**

180° − 96° = 84°; 84° ÷ 2 = 42°

Q3 **24**

Total marks scored = 34 × 4 = 136 so the final student score is 136 − 36 − 36 − 40 = 24

Test 13 answers continue on next page

Q4 $\frac{5}{14}$

3 tomatoes + 6 oranges + 5 bananas = 14 items

So probability of picking a banana = $\frac{5}{14}$

Q5 6

Can write out all the possibilities or use 3 × 2 × 1 = 6

Q6 **37 minutes**

17:57 → 18:34 is 37 minutes

Q7 157°

Sum of internal angles in pentagon = 540°

So fifth angle = 540° − 92° − 45° − 110° − 136° = 157°

Q8 £2·90

The difference between the 2 amounts is equivalent to 1 box and 1 drum.

So £9·90 − £7 = £2·90

Q9 34

59 − 25 = 34

Q10 **224 cm³**

Volume of 1 cube = 2 cm × 2 cm × 2 cm = 8 cm³

Volume of Figure 1 = 28 × 8 cm³ = 224 cm³

Test 14

Q1 34

Range is difference between 25°C and −9°C = 34°C

Q2 19

Difference between 12°C and −7°C = 19°C

Q3 −6

Mean = (−7°C + −9°C + −2°C) ÷ 3 = −18°C ÷ 3 = −6°C

Q4 15

40% of 25°C = 10°C; 25°C − 10°C = 15°C

Q5 12

The temperatures are all different.

Given the mode is 12°C, the temperature in Algiers must be 12°C

Test 15

Q1 434

7 × 2 = 14 cans per day; 31 days in July

31 × 14 = 434

Q2 317

Sum of internal angles in a pentagon = 540°

540° − 45° − 67° − 111° = 317°

Q3 30

8 ÷ 4 = 2 so 1 egg is required to bake a cake for 2 people

60 ÷ 2 = 30

Q4 3

Work backwards: 5th term = 42 so 4th term = (42 + 3) ÷ 3 = 15

Using same method, 3rd term = 6; 2nd term = 3

Q5 60

7 × 3 = 21 hours of work in total

So for 21 children, it will take 21 ÷ 21 = 1 hour = 60 minutes

Q6 126

P is smallest multiple of 6 greater than 122 so P = 126

Q7 12

Internal angle of equilateral triangle = 60°

$5x$ = 60 so x = 12

Q8 41

Paul takes 35 seconds; Henry takes 40 seconds; Max takes 48 seconds

Mean = (35 + 40 + 48) ÷ 3 = 41

Test 16

Q1 D

They write for 3·5 hours; Fabian: 3·5 × 64 = 224; Kate: 3·5 × 72 = 252

224 + 252 = 476

Q2 A

$(B \times 0) \div (9 + C) = 0 \div (9 + C) = 0$

Q3 B

At 2:07 p.m. there are 2 cells; at 2:14 p.m. there are 4 cells; at 2:21 p.m. there are 8 cells

Q4 E

7 years × 3 = 21 years; therefore, the combined age of the boys next year is 27 + 21 = 48

Q5 A

$K = \frac{1}{3} \times (600 \div 2) = 100$

So 100 = (4 × B^2) so 25 = B^2 so B = 5

$K + P − B$ = 100 + 2 − 5 = 97

Q6 A

3(2·75 cm² × 6) = 49·5 cm²

Q7 C

768 ÷ 8 = 96

Remember to add 1 more for the end so total is 97

Q8 B

4 Rogs = 32 Rigs; 2 Rigs = 9 Regs; 32 Rigs = 16 × 9 Regs = 144 Regs

Q9 D

Area = 2·25 cm² so each side = 1·5 cm

14 sides in total so perimeter = 14 × 1·5 cm = 21 cm

Test 17

Q1 273

Long division

Q2 176

X = 44 × 4 = 176

Q3 6

Volume of cube = 2 cm × 2 cm × 2 cm = 8 cm³

Volume of cuboid = 6 cm × 2 cm × 4 cm = 48 cm³

48 ÷ 8 = 6

Q4 105°

Y = 360° − 92° − 89° − 74° = 105°

Q5 32

5 p + 2 p = 7 p; 224 ÷ 7 = 32 so there must be 32 two-pence coins and 32 five-pence coins

Q6 (−7, 5)

Reflection in the y-axis means the x-coordinate changes from positive to negative.

Q7 **12 metres/hour**

20 cm/minute; 20 × 60 = 1,200 so 1,200 cm/hour so 12 metres/hour

Q8 2

```
    3  4  5
 +  2  8  7
   _____
    6  3  2
```

Q9   **4G − 14**

Perimeter = $2(G) + 2(G − 7) = 2G + 2G − 14 = 4G − 14$

Q10   **100°**

$100° + 64° + 16°$

Test 18

Q1   **987**

Using the 3 largest numbers in descending order.

Q2   **48,025**

Largest number using 5 cards is 98,764

Smallest number using 6 cards is 146,789

146,789 − 98,764 = 48,025

Q3   **9**

$9 × 1 = 9$

Q4   **147**

First 2 digits are the 2 smallest numbers, third digit is the next smallest odd number.

Q5 $\frac{1}{6}$

7 is the only prime number so 1 out of 6 = $\frac{1}{6}$

Test 19

Q1   **44**

$5^3 − 3^4 = (5 × 5 × 5) − (3 × 3 × 3 × 3) = 125 − 81 = 44$

Q2   **40**

10% of 7 kg = 700 g; 2,800 ÷ 700 = 4

So 2,800 g is 40% of 7 kg

Q3   **0·52**

Diameter = 2 × 3·25 = 6·5 cm

6·5 × 8 = 52 cm = 0·52 m

Q4 $\frac{1}{5}$

2 out of 10 are male so $\frac{2}{10} = \frac{1}{5}$

Q5   **50**

If 20% of X = 100 then X = 500; 10% of 500 = 50

Q6   **5**

$7(y + 8) = 91$ so $7y + 56 = 91$ so $7y = 35$ so $y = 5$

Q7   **15**

apples:oranges = 1:1·25 = 12(1):12(1·25) = 12:15

Q8   **4**

Set G = 1, 24, 2, 12, 3, 8, 4, 6

Set P = 1, 30, 2, 15, 3, 10, 5, 6

Numbers in P but not G: 30, 15, 10, 5 so 4 numbers in total

Test 20

Q1   **B**

28th May: 9 a.m. to end of day is 15 hours

29th May to 2nd June is 5 days, which equals 120 hours

3rd June: 12 a.m. to 2 a.m. is 2 hours

Total = 15 + 120 + 2 = 137 hours

Q2   **B**

1 book costs £42·42 ÷ 7 = £6·06

2 books cost £12·12; 3 books cost £18·18 so can only afford 2 books

Q3   **A**

Range = greatest − smallest = 9·999 − 9·889 = 0·11

Q4   **D**

Arrival time: 14:37; departure time of Train 2 is 17 minutes after 14:59, which is 15:16

14:37 to 15:16 is 39 minutes

Q5   **D**

$\frac{3}{8} + \frac{2}{5} = \frac{15}{40} + \frac{16}{40} = \frac{31}{40}$

So $\frac{9}{40}$ balls are green which is equal to 18 balls

So $\frac{1}{40}$ of the total is equal to 2 balls

$\frac{15}{40}$ balls are red; $\frac{15}{40} = 15 × \frac{1}{40}$; 15 × 2 = 30 balls

Q6   **C**

Cog 2 turns 27 times so Cog 1 turns (4 × 3) = 12 times

Cog 1 turns 8 times when Cog 3 turns 6 times

So when Cog 1 turns 12 times, Cog 3 must turn 9 times

Q7   **A**

$\frac{3}{4}$ of 3 litres = 2·25 litres = 2,250 ml

Total poured = 125 ml × 4 = 500 ml

Liquid left = 2,250 ml − 500 ml = 1,750 ml = 1·75 litres

Q8   **C**

After 2 stops, there are 6 fewer boys on the bus.

So there are 12 girls on the bus as there are twice as many girls after 2 stops.

Equal number of boys and girls to begin with so 12 girls and 12 boys.

Total = 12 + 12 = 24

Q9   **B**

Square side length = 20 ÷ 4 = 5 cm

Perimeter of rectangle is formed from 14 sides of the square.

14 × 5 = 70 cm

Test 21

Q1   **4·7152**

Subtraction

Q2   **48**

Difference between 6th term and 2nd term =

36 − 12 = 24

24 ÷ 4 = 6

So the difference between each term is 6 so 7th term = 42 and 8th term = 48

Q3   **11**

11 × 13 = 143

Q4   **6,156**

Second largest number = 9,735; smallest number = 3,579

9,735 − 3,579 = 6,156

Q5   **7·271**

$7\frac{1}{5} = 7·2$; $7\frac{8}{20} = 7·4$; $7\frac{1}{2} = 7·5$ so 7·271 is the closest

Q6   **£1·19**

Divide the total in two £2·56 ÷ 2 = £1·28

Divide the difference in two 18 p ÷ 2 = 9 p

Subtract the 9 p from £1·28 to find the amount Fred receives

£1·28 − £0·09 = £1·19

Q7   **933 g**

Weight of 10 shirts = 3,456 g − 346 g = 3,110 g

Weight of 1 shirt = 3,110 g ÷ 10 = 311 g

Weight of 3 shirts = 311 g × 3 = 933 g

Q8   **19**

6 people in front of her, 12 people behind her so 18 other people in the queue

18 + 1 = 19

Test 21 answers continue on next page

Q9 **32 cm**

Area of Triangle B = (base x height) ÷ 2

So 48 = 6h ÷ 2;

6h = 96; h = 16 cm

So height of Triangle C is 16 × 2 = 32 cm

Q10 **28**

37 × 28 = 1,036

Test 22

Q1 **135**

North to southeast clockwise is 135°

North to southeast anticlockwise is 225°

Q2 **315**

Northwest to west is 315°

Q3 **90**

John turns through 135°

Jim turns through 225°

225° − 135° = 90°

Q4 $\frac{5}{8}$

Full turn = 360°

$\frac{225}{360} = \frac{5}{8}$

Q5 **south**

540° = $1\frac{1}{2}$ turns so south

Test 23

Q1 **15**

39 ÷ 3 = 13 so numbers are 11, 13 and 15

Q2 **0·46**

All possible values of X round to 0·46 (2 d.p.)

Q3 **36**

Length is 9 cm so width is 4 cm

Area = 9 cm × 4 cm = 36 cm²

Q4 **16**

$4A = 80$; $B = 5$ so $80 = 16B$

Q5 **346**

7,024 − 6,678 = 346

Q6 **49**

3 largest prime numbers less than 20 are 19, 17 and 13

19 + 17 + 13 = 49

Q7 $\frac{5}{8}$

Simplifying $\frac{625}{1000}$ gives $\frac{5}{8}$

Q8 **93**

Volume of cube = 3 cm × 3 cm × 3 cm = 27 cm³

Volume of cuboid = 3 cm × 4 cm × 5·5 cm = 66 cm³

66 cm³ + 27 cm³ = 93 cm³

Test 24

Q1 **C**

1 m² = 100 cm × 100 cm = 10,000 cm²

Q2 **E**

Volume = area of circular face × height

= 7 cm × 2·75 cm² = 19·25 cm³

Q3 **D**

75% of 80 = 60; 60% of 60 = 36

Q4 **A**

$x^2 = 3^2 + 4^2$ so $x^2 = 9 + 16$ so $x^2 = 25$ so $x = 5$

Q5 **B**

$R = 360° − 90° − 89° − 134° = 47°$

Q6 **C**

Day 1 = X; Day 2 = $X + 10$; Day 3 = $X + 20$;

Day 4 = $X + 30$; Day 5 = $X + 40$

So $5X + 100 = 750$ so $5X = 650$ so $X = 130$

4th day = $X + 30 = 130 + 30 = 160$

Q7 **E**

Large fish scales = 9 × 400 = 3,600

Small fish scales = 8 × 200 = 1,600

Total scales = 3,600 + 1,600 = 5,200

Q8 **B**

Cube has 6 faces so $\frac{1}{2}$ of 1 face is $\frac{1}{12}$ of whole cube

so $1 − \frac{1}{12} = \frac{11}{12}$

Q9 **D**

As the second digit is 8 more than the first digit, the first digit must be 1 and the second digit must be 9. Therefore, the last digit is 4 so the number is 194.

Test 25

Q1 **1·5 litres**

8 parts in total; 2,000 ml ÷ 8 = 250 ml

So 6 parts = 250 ml × 6 = 1,500 ml = 1·5 litres

Q2 **405 cm²**

$\frac{2}{9}$ = 90 so $\frac{1}{9}$ = 45 so $\frac{9}{9}$ = 45 × 9 = 405 cm²

Q3 **£1·58**

The difference between the two is 3 carrots = 21 p

So 1 carrot = 7 p so 10 carrots = 70 p so 8 cucumbers and 12 potatoes = £3·85 − £0·70 = £3·16

So 4 cucumbers and 6 potatoes = £3·16 ÷ 2 = £1·58

Q4 **11**

21 × 21 = 441 and 31 × 31 = 961

So 21^2 → 31^2 = 11 square numbers

Q5 **5:16 p.m.**

2 p.m. to 5:30 p.m. = 3.5 hours

2 minutes slow every half an hour

So 14 minutes slow after 3.5 hours

14 minutes before 5:30 p.m. is 5:16 p.m.

Q6 **£10·80**

Cost = 12 × £0·6 = £7·20

Revenue = (6 × £1·20) + (6 × £1·80) = £7·20 + £10·80

= £18

Profit = Revenue − Cost = £18 − £7·20 = £10·80

Q7 **64 p**

50 p, 10 p, 2 p, 2 p

Q8 $\frac{1}{2}$

Outcomes are 1, 2, 3, 4, 5 and 6

2, 3 and 5 are prime so $\frac{3}{6} = \frac{1}{2}$

Q9 **106**

Rob scored 42 marks; Sarah scored $\frac{48}{2}$ = 24 marks;

Peter scored $\frac{5}{6}(48)$ = 40 marks

Total = 42 + 24 + 40 = 106 marks

Q10 **0**

Test 26

Q1 **56·25**

2·5 cm × 3 = 7·5 cm

Side length = 7·5 cm

Area = 7·5 cm × 7·5 cm = 56·25 cm²

Q2 **30**

7·5 cm × 4 = 30 cm

Q3   **4**

Figure 1 holds the same form 4 times when rotated 360°

Q4 $\frac{8}{9}$

8 of the 9 squares lie on the edge so $\frac{8}{9}$

Q5   **14**

9 1x1 squares; 4 2x2 squares; 1 3x3 square

9 + 4 + 1 = 14

Test 27

Q1   **58·63**

£53·30 × 10% = £5·33; £53·30 + £5·33 = £58·63

Q2   **4,320**

3 days = 3 × 24 hours = 72 hours

72 hours = 72 × 60 minutes = 4,320 minutes

Q3   **−29**

Lowest temperature = −3°C − 26°C = −29°C

Q4 $\frac{3}{8}$

$\frac{1}{2} \times \frac{3}{4} = \frac{3}{8}$

Q5   **18**

Q6   **14**

Y = 7 so $2Y$ = 14

Q7 $\frac{1}{24}$

$\frac{2}{48} = \frac{1}{24}$

Test 28

Q1   **C**

The shape has the same form when rotated 180°

Q2   **C**

$\frac{5}{8}$ = 0·625 so $1\frac{5}{8}$ = 1·625

Q3   **A**

180° − 73° = 107°

360° − 107° = 253°

Q4   **D**

7:4 → 11 parts; 44 ÷ 11 = 4 so there are (7 × 4) = 28 red and (4 × 4) = 16 green

Probability of choosing a red frog = $\frac{28}{44} = \frac{7}{11}$

Q5   **A**

1 p, 1 p, 1 p, 1 p, 1 p, 1 p, 1 p;

1 p, 1 p, 1 p, 1 p, 1 p, 2 p;

1 p, 1 p, 1 p, 2 p, 2 p;

1 p, 2 p, 2 p, 2 p;

1 p, 1 p, 5 p;

2 p, 5 p

Q6   **B**

8 cows eat 3 kg grass in 2 hours

So 8 cows eat 1·5 kg grass in 1 hour

So 24 cows eat 4·5 kg in 1 hour

Q7   **A**

The number must have a remainder of 4 when divided by 7

Q8   **D**

Let cost of strawberry = X so cost of apple = $2X$ and cost of orange = $4X$

$5X + 8X + 28X = 41X$

$41X$ = 82 p so X = 2 p

Q9   **C**

Shape B contains 16 small triangles so $\frac{1}{16}$ is shaded

Q10   **D**

There are 9 students between the 4th and the 14th on either side

So 9 + 9 + 2 = 20

Test 29

Q1   **34 minutes**

37 minutes after 3:36 is 4:13; 4:13 to 4:47 is 34 minutes

Q2   **588**

7 cows × 3 litres = 21 litres per day; 1 bottle = 250 ml so 21 × 4 = 84 bottles per day so 84 × 7 = 588 bottles per week

Q3   **224**

Work backwards: $\frac{1}{6}$ of 84 = 14; 4 × 14 = 56

The number is: 56 × 4 = 224

Q4   **24**

Lowest common multiple of 4, 6 and 8 = 24

Q5   **4·2368**

4·2458 → 4 is 0·2458; 4·2368 → 4 is 0·2368

3·7284 → 4 is 0·2716; 3·7232 → 4 is 0·2768

0·2368 is the smallest difference so 4·2368 is the closest to 4

Q6   **19·25 cm²**

2·5 cm² × 7 = 17·5 cm²; 10% of 17·5 cm² = 1·75 cm²

17·5 cm² + 1·75 cm² = 19·25 cm²

Q7   **563,250**

750 is half of 1,500 so 1,126,500 must also be halved to solve this: 751 × 750 = 1,126,500 ÷ 2 = 563,250

Q8   **£10·89**

£8·65 + £1·25 = £9·90; 10% of £9·90 = £0·99

£9·90 + £0·99 = £10·89

Q9   **£6·60**

£2·20 for first 20 minutes; 42 − 20 = 22 minutes left;

22 × £0·2 = £4·40

£2·20 + £4·40 = £6·60

Q10   **14**

2 + 5 + 20 = 27; 189 ÷ 27 = 7 so 7 of each coin so 2 p and 5 p total = 7 × 2 = 14

Test 30

Q1   **(3, −3)**

When reflecting in the x-axis, the y-coordinate is inverted. Point C = (3, 3) so x-axis reflection is (3, −3)

Q2   **(−3, −3)**

When reflecting in the y-axis, the x-coordinate is inverted. Point D = (3, −3) so y-axis reflection is (−3, −3)

Q3   **(−3, 3)**

Square has side length of 6 cm so point B = (−3, 3)

Q4   **18**

Each unit has width and length of 1 cm

Area = (base x height) ÷ 2 = (6 cm × 6 cm) ÷ 2 = 18 cm²

Q5   **9**

Area = (base x height) ÷ 2 = (3 cm × 6 cm) ÷ 2 = 9 cm²

Test 31

Q1   **30**

80% of 1,500 = 1,200 so 300 tickets remain

10% of 300 = 30

Q2   **216**

(16 × 6) + (8 × 7) + (8 × 8) = 216

Test 31 answers continue on next page

Q3 **6**

$(7F + 3F + 2F) \div 3 = 24$ so $12F = 72$ so $F = 6$

Q4 **16**

4 intervals between 1st and 5th terms; $28 \div 4 = 7$

so 3rd term = $2 + 7 + 7 = 16$

Q5 **49**

$\frac{2}{7} = 14$ so $\frac{1}{7} = 7$ so $\frac{7}{7} = 49$

Q6 **40**

7:3 means 7 out of 10 end in success so 70 successes and 30 failures

$70 - 30 = 40$

Q7 **16**

The expression $A + B = C$ can be rearranged to $C - B = A$

Since $C - 8 = A$ and $C - B = A$, B must equal 8

$AB = 56$ so $8A = 56$ so $A = 7$

$A + B = C$ so $7 + 8 = C$ so $C = 15$

$C + B - A = 15 + 8 - 7 = 16$

Test 32

Q1 **E**

2 m 43 cm equals 243 cm; $243 \div 3 = 81$

Q2 **C**

Cost of 1 theatre ticket = $5X$ so cost of 5 tickets = $25X$

Q3 **D**

32, 34, 36, 38

Q4 **A**

Harry = $3(X - 4) = 3X - 12$

Q5 **A**

$\frac{9}{1} + \frac{1}{9} + \frac{9}{1} = 18 + \frac{1}{9} = 18\frac{1}{9}$

Q6 **E**

$T < \frac{1}{6}$; $\frac{1}{8}$ is the only option less than $\frac{1}{6}$

Q7 **A**

Internal angle of pentagon = $540° \div 5 = 108°$

$V = 180° - 108° = 72°$

Q8 **B**

$3Y = 15$ so $Y = 5$; $2X - Y = 45$ so $2X = 50$ so $X = 25$

$Z + 25 + 5 = 60$ so $Z = 30$

Q9 **B**

$\frac{1}{4} \times \frac{1}{3} = \frac{1}{12}$

Test 33

Q1 **£24·30**

Cost = £45 + (£1·50 × 51) = £45 + £76·50 = £121·50

£121·50 ÷ 5 = £24·30

Q2 **21**

21 × 25 = 525

Q3 **15**

$20 \div 8 = 2.5$; $6 \times 2.5 = 15$

Q4 **64**

$x - 7 = 21$ so $x = 28$; $3y + 8 = 32$ so $3y = 24$ so $y = 8$

$2x + y = 2(28) + 8 = 56 + 8 = 64$

Q5 **690 cm**

Length of 1 side = 1,035 ÷ 3 = 345 cm

Length of 2 sides = 345 × 2 = 690 cm

Q6 **Kate**

Oldest to youngest: Alice, Amy, Ayesha, Kate, Linda

Q7 **$3 + 2F$**

Amelia = $F - 1$ so Esther = $5 + 2(F - 1) = 5 + 2F - 2 = 3 + 2F$

Q8 **502**

$3\frac{1}{3}$ hours = 200 mins; $2\frac{1}{5}$ hours is 132 mins

$2\frac{5}{6}$ hours = 170 mins

Total = 200 + 132 + 170 = 502 mins

Q9 **48**

$7 \rightarrow 8 = (7 \times 8) - 8 = 56 - 8 = 48$

Q10 **900 cm²**

Volume of 1 cube = 1,000 cm³ ÷ 8 = 125 cm³

Cube face length = $\sqrt[3]{125}$ = 5 cm

Surface area of 1 face = 5 cm × 5 cm = 25 cm²

Total number of faces = 36

36 × 25 cm² = 900 cm²

Test 34

Q1 **92·42**

Surface area = area of 2 heptagons + area of 7 rectangles

= (2 × 25·21 cm²) + (7(2 cm × 3 cm))

= 50·42 cm² + 42 cm²

= 92·42 cm²

Q2 **10**

Edges = 18; faces = 8; 18 − 8 = 10

Q3 **75·63**

Volume = cross-sectional area × height

So volume = 25·21 cm² × 3 cm = 75·63 cm³

Q4 **31**

Figure 1 has 9 faces; Figure 2 has 8 faces; Figure 3 has 14 faces

9 + 8 + 14 = 31

Q5 **69**

Figure 1 has 21 edges; Figure 2 has 18 edges; Figure 3 has 30 edges

21 + 18 + 30 = 69

Test 35

Q1 **9·10**

30% of £13 = £3·90; £13 − £3·90 = £9·10

Q2 **23**

Area = (base x height) ÷ 2 = $GU \div 2 = 46 \div 2 = 23$ cm²

Q3 **112**

Prime factors of 16 = 2 × 2 × 2 × 2

Prime factors of 14 = 2 × 7

so LCM = 2 × 2 × 2 × 2 × 7 = 112

Q4 **0·85**

$\frac{17}{20} = \frac{85}{100} = 0.85$

Q5 **462**

22 × 21 = 462

Q6 **90**

$\frac{70}{280} = \frac{1}{4}$; $\frac{1}{4}$ of 360° = 90°

Q7 **$\frac{3}{5}$**

$\frac{3}{4} \times \frac{4}{5} = \frac{12}{20} = \frac{6}{10} = \frac{3}{5}$

Q8 **250**

Area of field = 25 m × 30 m = 750 m²

$\frac{1}{3}$ not covered in grass

$\frac{1}{3} \times 750$ m² = 250 m²

Test 36

Q1   **C**

$B° = 180° - 42° - 39° = 99°$

Q2   **C**

Difference in sequence is −16, −15, −14 so next term is −13

$1,298 - 13 = 1,285$

Q3   **C**

December = 31 days

$31 × 7\frac{1}{2} = 232\frac{1}{2}$

Q4   **A**

A is the only option that can work if $P < 8$

Q5   **B**

Width = $(110 - 54 - 54) ÷ 2 = 2 ÷ 2 = 1$ cm

Area = $l × w = 54 × 1 = 54$ cm^2

Q6   **C**

Sum of angles in a triangle is 180°

If $W°$ is 63° then $U° = 180° - 54° - 63° = 63°$

However, $W°$ cannot equal $U°$ as this would make the triangle isosceles, and not scalene, so $W°$ cannot have a value of 63°

Q7   **B**

$10,000 × 0·002 × 7 = 20 × 7 = 140$

Q8   **A**

1:4 over 365 days means 73 cold days and 292 hot days

Q9   **D**

$T° + 2T° + 2T° + 4T° = 360°$ so $9T° = 360°$ so $T° = 40°$

Largest angle = $4T° = 160°$

Q10   **C**

The shape has 9 sides = nonagon

Test 37

Q1   **21,177**

$543 × 39 = 21,177$

Q2   **Wednesday**

21st August is a Sunday so 28th August is a Sunday so Sep 4th September is a Sunday so 7th September is a Wednesday

Q3   **north**

180° from southwest is northeast then turn 45° anticlockwise to north

Q4   **22·5 cm**

Figure 1 has 5 sides, each measuring 4·5 cm

4·5 cm × 5 = 22·5 cm

Q5   **1,103**

$27,575 ÷ 25 = 1,103$

Q6 $\frac{1}{2}$

2 out of the 4 numbers are the digit 4

So the probability of the number ending in 4 is $\frac{2}{4} = \frac{1}{2}$

Q7   **6·86**

$6\frac{5}{6} = 6.833...$; $6\frac{7}{8} = 6.875$

Q8   **107°**

A rhombus has 2 pairs of equal angles

$360° - 73° - 73° = 214°$; $214° ÷ 2 = 107°$

Q9   **1,000 cm³**

The width of the cube = twice radius of the sphere

Volume of cube = w × l × h = 10 cm × 10 cm × 10 cm = 1,000 cm³

Q10   **24**

The hexagon can be divided into 6 equilateral triangles, each with side 10 cm

Triangle B can fit into each of these triangles 4 times so it can fit 24 times in the hexagon

Test 38

Q1   **38**

Work backwards: 18 ÷ 3 = 6; 6 + 32 = 38

Q2   **48**

Work backwards: 39 − 27 = 12; 12 × 4 = 48

Q3   **16**

If $V = 33$ then $D = 3$; if $P = 8$ then $E = 29$

Mean = (29 + 3) ÷ 2 = 16

Q4   **−45**

17 − 32 = −15; −15 × 3 = −45

Q5   **0**

27 − 27 = 0; 0 × 4 = 0

Test 39

Q1   **50**

343 ÷ 7 = 49

1 more lamppost at the end so 49 + 1 = 50

Q2   **2·4**

$3 × \frac{4}{5} = \frac{12}{5} = 2\frac{2}{5} = 2.4$

Q3   **47**

Sequence is decreasing prime numbers so next term is 47

Q4   **6**

$B = 2T$; $T = 3K$ so $B = 2(3K) = 6K$ so six times

Q5   **0**

$4B + C = 20$; $B + C = 20$ so $4B = B$ so B must equal 0

Q6   **4**

676 ÷ 12 = 56 R 4

Q7   **07:36**

$6\frac{6}{8}$ hours = $6\frac{3}{4}$ hours = 6 hours 45 minutes so 07:36

Q8   **5**

Test 40

Q1   **D**

$\frac{4}{5}$ is equivalent to $\frac{32}{40}$ not $\frac{32}{42}$

Q2   **C**

Mean = (56 + 22 + 0 + 81) ÷ 4 = 159 ÷ 4 = 39·75

Q3   **E**

100 cm = 1 m; 72 km = 72,000 m; 72,000 ÷ 1 = 72,000 turns

Q4   **A**

Hexagons can be divided into 6 triangles each of area 6 cm^2 and height 3 cm

Base of triangle = 2(area) ÷ h = 12 ÷ 3 = 4 cm

Base of triangle = side length of hexagon

Figure A has 16 sides

Perimeter = 16 × 4 = 64 cm

Q5   **A**

1 mm × 500,000,000 = 500,000,000 mm = 50,000,000 cm = 500,000 m = 500 km

Q6   **E**

Ramp, floor and building form a triangle

Angle between ramp and wall = 180° − 23° − 90° = 67°

Test 40 answers continue on next page

Q7 **B**

7 dozen = 7 × 12 = 84; 42 nuts removed

Nuts remaining = $\frac{42}{84} = \frac{1}{2}$

Q8 **D**

Possible numbers: 3, 4, 6, 12

Q9 **C**

Number of edges = 20; number of faces = 10

20 × 10 = 200

Q10 **B**

$0.8 + \frac{3}{8} = 0.8 + 0.375 = 1.175$

Test 41

Q1 **54 cm²**

Area of 1 side = 3 cm × 3 cm = 9 cm²

Total surface area = 9 cm² × 6 = 54 cm²

Q2 **274,750**

Smallest possible population = 549,500

549,500 ÷ 2 = 274,750

Q3 **35 kph**

Speed = Distance ÷ Time = 140 ÷ 4 = 35 kph

Q4 $\frac{1}{2}$

C and D both equal 360° ÷ 5 = 72°

$(C \div 2) \div D = 36 \div 72 = \frac{1}{2}$

Q5 **24**

24 ÷ 7 = 3 R 3

Q6 **104**

Greatest two-digit prime number = 97

97 + 7 = 104

Q7 $G + 13$

Odd + Odd = Even

Q8 **5 8 4**

The sum of any 2 sides of a triangle must be greater than the 3rd side.

Q9 **75%**

2.5 kg cement and 7.5 kg gravel

7.5 kg of 10 kg is 75%

Q10 $T - 5U$

In total, she gives away $5U$ so she has $T - 5U$ left

Test 42

Q1 $\frac{2}{5}$

4 out of 10 are black so $\frac{4}{10} = \frac{2}{5}$

Q2 $\frac{1}{3}$

3 out of 9 are striped so $\frac{3}{9} = \frac{1}{3}$

Q3 $\frac{3}{10}$

6 out of 20 are white so $\frac{6}{20} = \frac{3}{10}$

Q4 $\frac{4}{25}$

$\frac{4}{10} \times \frac{4}{10} = \frac{16}{100} = \frac{4}{25}$

Q5 $\frac{2}{15}$

$\frac{4}{10} \times \frac{3}{9} = \frac{12}{90} = \frac{4}{30} = \frac{2}{15}$

Test 43

Q1 **150**

90 ÷ 60 = 1.5 so 150%

Q2 **100**

$\frac{1}{6}$ of an hour = 10 mins so $\frac{5}{6}$ of an hour = 50 mins

50 × 2 = 100

Q3 **504**

63 × 8 = 504

Q4 **2.625**

$\frac{3}{4}$ litre = 750 ml; $\frac{1}{2}$ of 750 ml = 375 ml

375 ml × 7 = 2,625 ml = 2.625 litres

Q5 **14**

2 × 14 = 28

Q6 **24**

360° ÷ 15 = 24°

Q7 **60**

30 + F = 32 so F = 2; 30F = B so 60 = B

Q8 **18**

12 km in 40 minutes so 3 km in 10 minutes so 18 km in 60 minutes

Test 44

Q1 **A**

4.5 km = 4,500 m; 4,500 ÷ 15 = 300 m

Q2 **C**

8✪ = (6 × 8) + 6 = 54

2✪ = (6 × 2) + 6 = 18

54 − 18 = 36

Q3 **A**

21:00 in Los Angeles is 06:00 in London

06:00 in London is 14:00 in Delhi

Q4 **C**

(8, 9) reflected in the x-axis is (8, −9)

(8, −9) reflected in the y-axis is (−8, −9)

Q5 **D**

$64 - 25 = 4^3 - 5^2 = 39$ so $c = 5$

Q6 **B**

28 sticks in collection so 47 − 28 = 19

Q7 **B**

23 numbers in total; 12 are even so $\frac{12}{23}$

Q8 **B**

$2(\frac{1}{2}(16(X))) = 16X$ so $16X = 64$ so $X = 4$

Q9 **C**

Morning temperature = −5°

Afternoon temperature = −5° + 12° = 7°

Night temperature = 7° − 17° = −10°

Test 45

Q1 **189**

180° − 117° = 63°; 63° × 3 = 189°

Q2 **1,080**

Sum of internal angles = 180° × (number of sides − 2) = 180° × 6 = 1,080°

Q3 **12**

Interior angle of Figure 2 is 108° so exterior angle = 72°

Interior angle of Figure 4 is 120° so exterior angle = 60°

72° − 60° = 12°

Q4 **8**

Figure 3 repeats its form 8 times when rotated 360°

Q5 **5**

Figure 4 has 6 lines of symmetry

Figure 1 has 1 line of symmetry

6 − 1 = 5